REPORTING ON COLOMBIA

ALSO BY JULIÁN ESTEBAN TORRES LÓPEZ

Ninety-Two Surgically Enhanced Mannequins:
A Micro-Poetry Collection

Marx's Humanism and Its Limits:
Why Marx Believed We Should Achieve Socialism
and Communism Nonviolently

REPORTING ON COLOMBIA

Essays on Colombia's History, Culture, Peoples, and Armed Conflict

Julián Esteban Torres López

The Nasiona

San Francisco

ISBN-13: 978-1-950124-06-0

For more information, contact

Nasiona.mail@gmail.com

https://thenasiona.com

https://jetorreslopez.com

Cover photograph is of an angry mob reacting to the assassination of populist Liberal Party leader Jorge Eliécer Gaitán, 10 April 1948. The assassination on the streets of Bogotá is referred to as El Bogotázo, which led to a 10-year internal, bloody strife called La Violencia. The result of this violent period gave rise to the armed conflict Colombia continues to experience today.

Author photograph by Joanna Staniszewski.

Contents

Introduction

The morning after my birth, the front page of *The New York Times* did not greet my parents as it normally would have if they had remained immigrants in Queens, New York. The newspaper would have showcased a photo of the Pope kissing the foreheads of African children, another photo of Atlanta residents mourning the killings of their own boys and girls, and a lead article about how the Soviet Defense Minister said the West was trying to reopen the Cold War.

Instead, Colombian newspapers hailed my parents with headlines in Medellín that recounted hunger strikes and plastered photographs that would prove how some now-forgotten dissident was tortured. If I was born literate and read those front pages, I would not have had high hopes for my brown-skinned life.

I didn't know it then, but I was born into an armed conflict spanning centuries, whose roots are still entangled in the colonial mindset and situations we inherited after liberation from Spain. Though Spanish rule ended, control of land, resources, and peoples remained in the hands of the élite. The numerous civil wars we Colombians have experienced are simply different manifestations of the same root causes.

As a result, prolonged war has drained Colombia of its most essential natural and human resources and has created an aggressive and vengeful environment of resentment and resistance. Though the second oldest democracy in the hemisphere, an effective modern nation-state has never existed here. Its 200+ years of so-called democracy have been a farce given Colombia's feudalist innards and fascist corporatism exoskeleton.

Further, the continuing armed conflict is exacerbated by the country's historical lack of hegemony, institutionalized and systemic violence, corruption, socio-political exclusion, lack of social mobility opportunities, and foreign intervention. We must curb the traditional might-makes-right conflict resolution methods and the state must gain true legitimacy if Colombians are ever to manifest their potential.

In this book, I machete through the tall weeds of Colombia's power vacuum and fragmented sovereignty, peel away the layers of the country's flirtation with modernity and class consciousness, dissect the insecurity of Colombia's security policies, and look to understand who and what stand in the way of Colombia becoming the El Dorado it could become.

Included in this collection are 17 essays I wrote between 2008 and 2013. It was the period of my life when I was the most prolific and dedicated to unearthing the soil that nourished the roots of Colombia's armed conflict.

During this period, I worked as a researcher on several political science projects alongside Dr. James F. Rochlin. The work with which I assisted him resulted in his publication of a book and several peer-reviewed articles in academic journals. The publications dealt with topics of Canada's human rights impact assessment and the free trade agreement with Colombia, the negative impact of petroleum production in the Ecuadorian

Amazon bordering Colombia, the challenges of security in Colombia, and the political economy of strategic conflict between Venezuela and Colombia. I also taught university courses on comparative politics and issues in South American politics at University of British Columbia Okanagan during this time, where I was a Ph.D. candidate exploring how foreign intervention and multinational corporations exacerbated the Colombian armed conflict.

I share here three unpublished long-form academic essays, one of which I presented at the 2010 Congress of the Latin American Studies Association in Toronto, Canada, for the panel called "Latin American Foreign Policies: South America and the U.S." The other two essays are the evolved manifestations of ideas that were budding within me when I was a panelist at a public workshop entitled "Colombia, the Conflicts, and Beyond: Perspectives on a Canadian Ally," held in Vancouver, Canada, in 2009, and sponsored by Simon Fraser University—ideas I later developed and which became the foundation for an unfinished doctoral dissertation manuscript.

The other 14 essays I share here appeared in their initial forms in *Colombia Reports*, the country's largest independent news source in English. I wrote them when I was a columnist for the publication. The essays are grounded in my grant- and fellowship-funded research during those years. The column provided me the opportunity to explore the armed conflict as well as other issues that interested me about my natal land, such as our history, culture, and diverse peoples.

With all 17 essays, I also shine a light on the roots of Colombian consciousness and the frameworks of Colombian society—its backdrop, social structures, agents, institutions, systems, unspoken assumptions, dominant culture, and taken-for-granted ideologies that pass as common sense.

During my research, I tracked down the newspapers published on the date of my birth—the ones from where I was nearly born (Queens) and the ones where I was born (Medellín). I was surprised, but not shocked, to find that the headlines of that day could have been written almost four decades later, today. It's difficult to stay hopeful regarding the armed conflict when the history of Colombia has been drenched in exploitation and blood from the very beginning. It's difficult to stay hopeful when the main causes of such incessant violence and injustice are never sincerely or effectively tackled.

If we ever want to live the dream of potentially becoming the El Dorado we could become and to create a truly American (as in, of the Americas) artifact of humanity and liberty, then we must choose to unify. We must stop passing the buck of responsibility. We must stop supporting policies and institutions and systems that ostracize, stigmatize, and dehumanize our neighbors, our brothers and sisters, and policies that unequivocally support the instrumentalization and exploitation of our very selves.

Colombia has a lot to celebrate. We Colombians have a rich, multicultural history of plurality of identities and traditions. Our many carnivals and festivals—one for every day of the year—are testament to a rich culture. But this does not mean the dream has been fully realized. I hope I get to see the day when the newspaper headlines no longer remind me of my birth.

Julián Esteban Torres López

5 September 2019

What Does It Mean to Be Colombian?

19 October 2010, *Colombia Reports*

There are over 45 million "Colombians" living within the country's borders and about 5 million abroad. I am said to fall under the latter category. However, of these 50+ million individuals, can we really sit down and agree on a set of characteristics to essentialize what it means to be a Colombian?

Though it seems easy enough for those who consider themselves Colombian, once challenged to unpack what it means most will recognize there are inherent limitations to this endeavor as there are any time one tries to essentialize anything. In the process of trying to construct an identity, one always leaves something out when trying to include something else.

Am I Colombian if I don't eat bandeja Paisa since I'm a vegetarian? Am I Colombian if I am an atheist and over 90% of Colombians believe in some kind of deity (mostly of the Roman Catholic variety)? Am I Colombian if I am against bull fighting because of its inherent animal cruelty for the sake of human entertainment? What if I am for gay marriage, stem cell research, and abortion? Am I Colombian if I find aguardiente disgusting and I don't drink coffee? What if I can't dance cumbia? What if I am against both Uribe *and* the FARC?

Or, do I just have to be born within the county's borders, regardless of my opinions on the issues delineated above? I was born in Medellín, Antioquia, but am I a Paisa? I have only lived in Colombia for about third of my life. I speak Spanish but am not considered by home-grown "Colombians" as one of "them" because I have been away for too long and have gathered different experiences "they" don't share. Sometimes, I am considered a gringo, but in the United States, I am occasionally regarded as a spic or an alien. I am a stranger in my homeland, and everywhere else I have lived (U.S., Canada, Chile, and Japan) I am not identified as one of them, either. In fact, racist comments aside, I am mostly regarded as "Colombian" abroad, even though I now also have a U.S. passport.

How about our blood? Is there really such a thing as being 100% Colombian? If anything, the Amerindians of pre-Columbian Colombia may have been closer to this than us, but even they were descendants of indigenous peoples who migrated south from Asia and Central and North America. Where do we draw the line?

Post-colonialism, the genetic make-up of what it means to be a Colombian has also been mixed with European and West African blood and the genes from others who have immigrated to the territory. We also have to recognize much Spanish blood, for example, is not just European, but also Middle Eastern and North African. All one must do is study the great wars of the Iberian Peninsula, the region, and their migrants, of the last 2,000+ years, to trace the lineage of much of Colombia's ancestors. This may explain why others have many times mistaken me for indigenous, Mediterranean, and Middle Eastern. Understanding such genetic history, it becomes difficult to suggest there is such a thing as someone who is 100% Colombian. In the process of trying to construct this identity, we are sure to leave someone out.

When I left Medellín as a child during the violent years of Pablo Escobar's total war against the government, I was transplanted to a new country without knowing the culture or language. My sister and I were two of fewer than a handful of students who spoke Spanish in our new school. Being thrown into this new world, I, like many who may have shared the experience, searched for an identity. I adopted "Colombian." Nevertheless, for the sake of staying under the radar, the name on my Colombian birth certificate became anglicized and shortened from four names to two. "You're no longer Julián Esteban Torres López, but [insert American English accent here] Julian Torres," I remember my father telling me this when we left Colombia and tried to survive as "illegal aliens" for over a decade.

With Colombia's tainted international reputation, I was bombarded by the essentialization of "Colombians" from "non-Colombians." Every chance I got, I took the opportunity to challenge their stereotypes and prejudices: "No, my father is not a drug dealer ... No, we actually do have paved roads ... No, I don't drink coffee ... No, I've never killed anybody." In the U.S., I became an ambassador for Colombia and "Colombians" as an adolescent. Hollywood and the news made it difficult to grow up without being negatively portrayed by those who had never met me or "my people." As an adult, I've come to realize that this unwanted ambassadorship led me to become a scholar in Colombian culture, politics, and history.

As I spoke with other immigrants around the world, I became aware we shared a similar experience. We tended to feel more "Colombian" than possibly those living back home. What exactly that meant, I don't know. We, in a way, embraced other stereotypes of what a "Colombian" supposed to be. This may have been due to the fear of losing one's language, traditions, and culture while abroad, which led us to cling on to that abstract and somewhat imaginary identity maybe stronger than non-immigrants. For a while in my 20s, I even tried to name myself and claim myself—as Khalil Gibran once wrote—by readopting my Spanish name in pronunciation, spelling, and number of given names. This confused my friends, and, though satisfied me for a while, still left an emptiness inside because, as I have come to realize, I am more than just the X identity I tried to be. Instead of toeing the line of some abstract notion, I was who I was: a hybrid, mixed.

It was not until last year, when a friend asked me the following questions, that I began to really dissect my identity: "Are you proud to be a Colombian? Are you proud of Colombia?" I don't recall my exact answer, but I have since meditated heavily on this topic. Though for years I was a self-proclaimed ambassador for Colombia and Colombians, I quickly realized I was not in standing to answer such questions. Could I really take praise or blame for what Colombians have done, good or bad?

Maybe we cannot sit down and come up with a list of characteristics that essentializes 50+ million people. Maybe it is more like Ludwig Wittgenstein's idea of family resemblance: there is no one characteristic we all share, but if studied as a group we can conclude we are most definitely related. Or, maybe it is like what the U.S. Supreme Court says about pornography: though we can't agree on one definition, we know it when we see it.

All I know is that in three decades of reflecting on my so-called identity, I have come to accept that answering the question guiding this discussion on what it means to be Colombian is both personal and communal in nature. There seems to be a need or want to define others and ourselves to more effectively realize the lives we wish to lead as individuals and as collectives. Further, the answers seem to suggest it is not a black or white issue. There's a continuum, a liminal space, where all of us fall between the affirmative YES and the affirmative NO. It is in this arena where "boundaries dissolve a little and we stand there, on the threshold, getting ourselves ready to move across the limits of what we were into what we are to be."

My identity is a hybrid cluster of my own experiences. Friedrich Nietzsche may have said it best when he wrote, in *Thus Spoke Zarathustra: A Book for All and None*, the following:

> I am a wanderer and mountain climber,
> he said to his heart,
> I do not love the plains,
> and it seems I cannot sit still for long.
> And whatever may still overtake me as fate and
> experience—
> it will be a wandering and a mountain climbing;
> in the end one experiences only oneself.

Colombia, 1757: Birthplace of America's Abolition of Slavery?

26 Aug 2010, *Colombia Reports*

Two score and seven years ago, Martin Luther King, Jr., delivered his famous "I Have a Dream Speech" on the steps of the Lincoln Memorial. On August 28, the 47th anniversary of King's plea for equality and an end to discrimination, Colombians continue to call for the realization of their own dreams. The sweltering summer of our legitimate discontent will not pass until there is an invigorating autumn.

King had prepared a text when he took the steps of the Lincoln Memorial, but what has become known to the world as the "I Have a Dream Speech" was partially improvised from bits of wisdom and cries for liberty from his previous speeches. If you watch King deliver the speech you can see when he begins to depart from the prepared text. Some say what may have prompted this spontaneous outpouring was a call from

Mahalia Jackson to "Tell them about the dream, Martin!" The public declaration of his dream came from the calls of others who shared his vision.

These calls united a collective dissatisfaction that, on the steps of the Lincoln Memorial, had already culminated into a mass movement of non-violence and civil disobedience, and forced the country and the world to take notice. As King once said, "Freedom is never voluntarily given by the oppressor; it must be demanded by the oppressed." But such demands do not have to be violent in nature. As his civil rights movement demonstrated, the collective consciousness of a people—who came together, in concert, to stop cooperating with the unjust actions and policies of an oppressive regime—can transform a nation. Less than two months after King publicly proclaimed the collective dream of millions of U.S. citizens, the U.S. Congress passed a bill of civil rights into law.

Ten score and six years prior to the U.S. Congress legitimizing King's dream, some African and Afro-descendant slaves in Colombia may have been heard singing words similar to the old Negro spiritual, "Free at last! Free at last! Thank God Almighty, we are free at last!" The rest of the world was slow to respond to such wails and waves of jubilation.

England made its first judgment in 1772 (the Somersett's Case) that held slavery to be unlawful. Thousands of slaves were soon emancipated. Haiti's slave rebellion, which focused on expelling French colonizers, did not start until 1791. By 1804, after much bloodshed, Haiti had become the first independent nation in Latin America and the first post-colonial independent nation led by blacks in the world. Haiti's national constitution of 1801 is considered one of the earliest progressive human rights documents ever declared by a nation. It even affirmed plans to import foreign slaves into Haiti to later free them. In 1808, the United States took steps to ban the importation of African slaves.

11

But in 1757 Colombia, freedom rang from the mountainside of Eastern Antioquia in the town of El Retiro. Thirty-three kilometers from Medellín, you can find this historic town, known both for its mining and its history of liberty. As some locals, like Lazarito, have claimed, "It is a town of poor people surrounded by the rich, a symbiosis between a rich population and freed slaves." In doing research for this article, I came across three different popular historical interpretations of the actual formal act of releasing Black folks from slavery by granting them liberty in El Retiro.

One account by Javier Ocampo López, in his book *Mitos y Leyendas de Antioquia la Grande (Myths and Legends of Antioquia la Grande)* describes how in 1757 some 127 African slaves were freed by an Antioquian widow, doña Javiera Londoño. This was the first time this occurred in all of the Americas in the 18th century. The sculpture in the photo above symbolizes this occasion. Londoño—a woman, let's not forget—may have become Colombia's and America's (North, Central, and South) first true slave liberator: ¡La Libertadora!

Ocampo recounts that doña Londoño and her husband, Sergeant Ignacio Castañeda, were known for being kind and affectionate to their slaves, and ensured to take care of them. Social justice, it is said, was very important to the couple. When Londoño's husband died, la doña granted liberty to all her slaves.

Another account is chronicled in the book *Solo quiero que me escuche: Cronicas del Oriente antioqueño y la subregion Nus* (*I just want you to listen to me: Chronicles of the Antioquian East and the Nus subregion*) where historian Marta Agudelo de Pelaez's version of the Castañeda Londoño family's act of manumission is recounted. According to Agudelo, in 1734, El Retiro's subsoil natural resources, such as gold, quartz, and salt, seduced doña Londoño and her husband. They soon began to exploit the mines with the help of their African slaves. Due to hardships and the high costs of maintaining slaves, the couple had to liberate 32 slaves. Agudelo agrees with Ocampo that this was the first time in the Americas when African slaves were formally awarded their freedom.

Christopher Cameron, historian and expert on the African slave trade and anti-slavery movements, confirms this fact. In my interview with Dr. Cameron, he said that prior to 1757, there were no legal cases of manumission in the Americas. There were, however, many cases of marronage in "South America and Jamaica where a large number of slaves ran away together and ended up signing deals with their former masters, in effect freeing them." The closest case to something that resembles manumission was in Massachusetts when in 1700 a court granted a slave, Adam Saffin, his freedom after "he sued his master, John Saffin, because he claimed he had been promised his freedom." However, this was not a case of liberation for so-called humanitarian purposes, as some claim the El Retiro story to be.

El Retiro's main courtyard blends both Ocampo's and Agudelo's accounts. On 27 December 2007, the town mayor inaugurated a monument to both la doña and the sergeant for liberating 127 of their slaves. The sculpture itself is of doña Londoño cutting a slave loose from his tied wrists. The following 1757 testament, which you can find on a plaque at the foot of the monument, however, is attributed to both la doña and the sergeant: "I give them liberty in every form of right that free people who are not subject to slavery have, and may they do whatever free people want to do and should do."

Though this selective act of manumission did not make a difference in the larger scheme of things (as far as national policy was concerned, since Colombia did not realize the full abolition of slavery until the following century), it did make a difference to those formerly enslaved. The act also set the foundation that helped change public perception as to who should be regarded as a human being and who deserved to be treated with full dignity and respect. Though some question the motivation for freeing the Londoño and Castañeda slaves—I'm on this camp since this historical account appears to be whitewashed—the fact remains the slaves were freed, and in doing so the two set an example. Maybe this is how the legend of El Retiro should be remembered and honored by all Colombians, not just those of African descent?

Ocampo wrote that the "liberated slaves were given the surname Castañeda and committed themselves to annually celebrate" their freedom. Toward the end of the year, in December, the former slaves would find their way to their former town to reunite and commemorate their *retirement* from slavery. For this reason, the town is called El Retiro. The yearly celebration of the new Castañeda family was the origin for what Colombians now know as the "Fiesta de los Negritos." But maybe what we should also acknowledge is the white supremacy the sculpture represents. The monument praises the so-called kindness of a slave master and not the slaves. The monument is centered around honoring the victimizer, not commemorating the woes of the slaves. This is one of the most extreme and clearest examples of white saviorhood I have ever seen memorialized.

I am breaking from tradition today and instead of celebrating this story only in late December and early January to coincide with the Fiesta, I am narrating it now to parallel the proclamation of King's "I Have a Dream Speech," because the two stories complement one another. It is time to commemorate Colombia's heritage, and also a time for further dreaming and critical thinking.

The promissory note of equality to which every Colombian was to fall heir via the 1991 constitution has been a "bad check." This bad check has been returned to the people marked as "insufficient funds," because of the country's inability—as a collective—to live up to the spirit of the law and its obligations. Those armed groups—like the Colombian armed forces, paramilitaries, guerrillas, and drug cartels—who have supposedly fought for a unified Colombia, for human dignity, for the life, liberty, and the pursuit of happiness of ALL Colombians, have tried incessantly to manifest a grandiose Colombia in botched attempts.

Why has this been the case? In their militarized quest for unity, they have justified the extermination of a segment of the Colombian population, each armed group with a different targeted "lesser human" who can be disposed off without guilt. In the words of James Madison, we cannot unify a country by means of a cure that is worse than the disease itself. The justification of violence to achieve certain ends is drastically undermined if those ends cannot even be guaranteed.

As Hannah Arendt so eloquently put it in her classic *On Violence*,

> The very substance of violent action is ruled by the means-end category, whose chief characteristic, if

15

applied to human affairs, has always been that the end is
in danger of being overwhelmed by the means which it
justifies and which are needed to reach it. Since the end
of human action, as distinct from the end products of
fabrication, can never be reliably predicted, the means
used to achieve political goals are more often than not
of greater relevance to the future world than the
intended goals.

Colombians have fallen to the wildfires of violence that have
plagued the country and its people for far too long.
Colombians are chained to the very means they justify to bring
them liberty. Colombians are chained to their own inability to
find creative, peaceful conflict resolution solutions.
Colombians are chained to labels that dehumanize and taunt.
Colombians are chained to themselves and to the devises of
their own choosing. Colombian institutions have chosen
violence. To take up arms is a choice, not a pre-determined,
mechanical, fated act. If Colombians—regardless of skin color,
regardless of religion, regardless of political affiliation,
regardless of level of education and class, and regardless of
sexual orientation—want to live the dream of the Castañeda
family and El Retiro, they must choose to do so and help make
it so for the vulnerable sectors of our society.

If Colombians ever want to live the dream Simón Bolívar left
behind as a truly American artifact of humanity and liberty,
then we must choose to unify. We must stop passing the buck
of responsibility. We must stop supporting policies that
ostracize, stigmatize, and dehumanize our neighbors, our
brothers and sisters, policies that unequivocally support the
instrumentalization of our very selves.

As Bolívar's dream dictated,

To extricate our nascent republic from this chaos, not
even the full weight of our moral faculties will suffice
unless we can learn to unify our country: its
governmental structure, its legislative body, and its

16

national spirit. Unity, unity, unity—that must be our
motto. If the blood of our citizens is diverse, let us make
it one. If our constitution has divided the powers, let us
unify them. If our laws are moribund relics of every
ancient and modern despotism, let us tear down this
monstrous edifice and, obliterating even its ruins, build
a temple of justice in whose sacred precincts we can
dictate a ... code of law.

On this day of tribute and remembrance, let us honor not only
Dr. King, not only a dream, but a possibility. The U.S. civil
rights movement provided evidence that extending civil rights
may be achievable through peaceful measures. The legend of
Antioquia's El Retiro has provided Colombians an example
that one does not have to wait for an army or a guerrilla to win
a war, or for a government to make justice into law for wrongs
to be righted. The people, too, have power do to so, as
demonstrated by Dr. King, as demonstrated by la doña and her
sergeant. As Gandhi claimed, be the change you want to see in
the world. Don't wait for it to happen. Act.

Colombia has a lot to celebrate. Colombians have a rich, multicultural history of a plurality of identities and traditions. Our
many carnivals and festivals—one for every day of the year, as
the "Colombia is Passion" commercial proudly boasts—are
testament to a rich culture. But this does not mean the dream
has been fully realized. I hope I get to see the day when the
entirety of Colombia can be recognized as El Nuevo Retiro. I
await such a glorious moment.

The sweltering summer of our legitimate discontent will not
pass until there is an invigorating autumn. Patiently, I wait for
a change of season.

Plato in Pre-Columbian Colombia?

31 August 2010, *Colombia Reports*

Hypothesis: *Plato was in pre-Columbian America!*
Suggestion: *We should start looking in Santa Marta, Colombia, for his footprints!*

The above claims may sound ludicrous. Nevertheless, I am quite certain I have found the influence of Plato's thought in an indigenous Colombian civilization.

Let us be clear from the outset: I am not the first to suggest such a shocking claim. Previous theories of encounters between the native peoples of the Americas and those across the Atlantic and the Pacific have been numerous. Below are seven of the most common theories:

(1) There is a large boulder some 20 miles west of Popayan, Colombia, in a wilderness named La Yunga, carved with symbols. Father Leopoldo von Kinder, a former professor, deciphered and identified the markings some 80 years ago as Phoenician, dating from 180 to 202 BCE.

(2) Not much is known about the people who built the mysterious statues of San Agustin—the largest group of religious monuments and megalithic sculptures in South America. Some experts claim the area was settled 5,300 years ago. Because of the musical instruments some of the statues seem to be playing—instruments only found in other parts of the world before the San Agustin civilization disappeared during the 15th century—other experts suggest these people were either influenced by or were Asian, Hindu, or Egyptian.

(3) Some, like Gavin Menzies, in his book *1421: The Year China Discovered the World*, claim Chinese DNA has been found among native peoples of Colombia, and that similar DNA can be found up and down the Pacific coast of the Americas.

(4) Erik von Däniken, the controversial Swiss author, is known for his outrageous claims that extraterrestrials influenced ancient civilizations and cultures, like the San Agustin civilization.

(5) Others claim there is a presence in Oceania of several cultivated plant species native to South America, and that domesticated chickens were introduced to the continent via Polynesia, South Pacific. All of this, it is said, occurred before Columbus.

(6) Most widely known is the Bering Strait Theory: ancient peoples from Asia traversed the Bering Strait between what are now Russia and Alaska. These people then migrated south, and Colombia saw the continent's first inhabitants arrive between 12,500 and 70,000 years ago.

(7) Others have suggested that white men had been to Latin America before Columbus. Many of the major pre-Columbian civilizations believed there would be a return of white-skinned gods, and because of this legend many indigenous peoples were caught off-guard when the European white men landed

on their shores and conquered them. These legends, in a land where white skin was nonexistent, imply previous contact with Europeans.

To these theories I add my own by proposing there is evidence the Kogi indigenous people of Colombia (direct descendants of the great Tayrona civilization) were influenced by the ideas of Plato's work, *The Republic*, in their culture and the way they organized their economy and politics, even before Spanish conquest. The similarities between Plato's ideal society and the Kogi's real one are surely too close to have occurred by mere coincidence, especially since no society in history has ever come close to resembling Plato's republic. The similarities are uncanny.

This is not an academic paper, so I won't go into extreme detail. Those who want to explore the similarities for themselves should start by reading Plato's *Republic,* then Alan Ereira's *Elder Brothers* on the Kogi (or check out Ereira's film documentary, *From the Heart of the World: The Elder Brothers' Warning*).

You can take my word for it or do your own analysis, but I am left stunned by the similarities between Plato's ideal society and the Kogi way of life, as if Plato's metaphors and allegories were taken literally and put into practice. If you have ever learned a second language, you may be able to relate to the experience of taking expressions at face value when, in reality, they have metaphorical meaning. The fact Kogi way of life literally exemplifies Plato's ideas suggests the Kogi could have learned such ethics from foreigners whose main language was not a variation of Chibcha native tongue. I suggest one of two things: the ideals of Plato's republic may have influenced the Kogi in deep ways, or the Kogi came up with these remarkable philosophical and ethical practices on their own. I hope—and it is more likely—the latter is true.

20

For me, this is the real El Dorado! The two lost cities are both in Colombia. The lost city of the Muisca civilization is the source of the legend of El Dorado, while the lost city of the Tayrona civilization (the most important archaeological "discovery" in Latin America of the 20th century) is where the Kogi people reside.

El Dorado for the Spaniards was simply a place to pillage for its material wealth—the open vein of the Americas, as Eduardo Galeano once wrote. In contrast, the Kogi people are the real El Dorado, because they are a living and thriving example of a semi-utopian society. A utopian society, by definition, does not and cannot exist. This suggests true harmony and peace among people, through politics, as Plato suggested, is not utopian, but possible. (Of course, however, what a utopian society is for one culture may be different to another and may even change within the same culture given that utopian ideas tend to be tied to social constructs.) What is even more remarkable, however, is the Kogi's way of life has mostly remained untainted and peaceful after centuries of being surrounded by the most violent of the region's conflicts: Colombia.

Though it is important to see the connection between Plato and the Kogi, the real purpose here is not merely pedantic, and I am aware my initial claims are speculative. What I hope to achieve with this discussion is that by linking Plato's articulation of an ideal society to the Kogi of the Colombian Sierra Nevada Mountains of Santa Marta, we can start to recognize that the lives we may want to lead are more possible than we thought. Further, we should not overlook the inherent, systemic racism in many of the hypotheses I outlined above that suggest there is no way native peoples of the Americas could have ever been intelligent enough to create so-called "civilized" things. This idea that there is just no way the "savages" of the Americas could have done all they did on their own—so, therefore, some other civilized people must have

21

come to civilize the natives—is disgusting. Think about it, people are more apt to believe extra-terrestrials must have influenced such ancient civilizations instead of accepting that maybe brown and black people outside of Europe could be intelligent and creative enough to build and create the great and awe-inspiring things they did.

A further purpose that grows from the previous one is that maybe instead of looking at an ancient Greek philosopher who lived over 2,400 years ago, we can begin to look inwardly more intensely, at ourselves, presently and historically, for an example of how we can organize our societies to fulfill human needs and concerns more effectively.

It makes sense to go to the most peaceful people in the world to learn how to be peaceful, while simultaneously studying the most violent to see what the reasons and causes may be for such violence.

If Plato were alive today, he may have claimed the Kogi are closely aligned to his ideal republic. If this is the case, and we currently look to Plato's republic to educate ourselves about politics, then why not look at the Kogi and try to learn from these *living* ancient people with even more vigor than we study Plato, since Plato just philosophized while the Kogi actualize?

In fact, if we can remove the unwarranted and ingrained prejudice that only the West is civilized, we may be able to start looking within at the history, cultures, economies, and politics of those once (and often still) viewed as savages, barbarians, and uncivilized peoples not only for knowledge (e.g., how the Egyptians built the pyramids) but wisdom: the ability to optimally apply knowledge to produce desired ends.

A society that neglects its elders sacrifices its future.

We will continue to sacrifice Colombia's unless we start to include other voices, such as the Kogi's, such as the indigenous Minga. The perspectives of these elder brothers and sisters do not have much weight in Colombian democracy, since they account for less than 1% of the country's population. We need to take deliberate action to listen and learn. They have been here longer than we have. They have something to offer.

Though many elders of the world are no longer with us, many still walk among us. We should become more curious about the centuries and millennia of wisdom passed down from all parts of the world, not just the ancient Greeks or the immature U.S., for example. The more we do this, the more we will be able to generate our desired actions and results, and, thus, increase the probability of a more positive future for us all.

I will say it again, a society that neglects its elders sacrifices its future.

It is time to listen before we drive them, and the rest of Colombia, into extinction. It's time to listen before even our own footprints become archaeological artifacts for post-Colombian civilizations.

Escobar & bin Laden: Bigger Than the Man

5 May 2011, *Colombia Reports*

Though there are differences between the two men, I liken Osama bin Laden's death with Pablo Escobar's in 1993. Both were the most wanted men in the world. Both were considered narco-terrorists. Both were a threat to U.S. interests. The U.S. also benefited at certain times from these men. There was a long manhunt for both men. The U.S. was involved in killing both men.

If we could learn anything from these past 18 years after Escobar's death, what could that be? Killing one man at the head of something that is bigger than the man does not make the issue go away, especially if the root problems are not tackled. Eighteen years have passed and the so-called war on drugs (now a narco-terrorist war since 9/11) continues. It has evolved.

Strategies changed when new leaders took charge after Escobar's murder. Because of context and changing environmental drifts, not only did strategies and tactics change but new actors also got involved—some more, some less, some new. The drug war/narco-terrorist war continues 18 years later. In fact, it has been in the U.S. for a while not only via consumption of the products, but the violence is closer than ever—arriving to territorial U.S. by means of the U.S.-Mexico border, for example.

If we continue with outdated strategies and tactics, we will continue with similar results, as the drug war in the Americas is testament. Killing the head of one of the most profitable markets in the world (though illicit), as was the case with Escobar, will not cut demand for the product. In turn, some other businessperson will most likely take the shoes of the previous one who was killed, like if the CEO of an oil company would be replaced if he, too, passed away unexpectedly.

Though he was the orchestrator of 9/11, Al Quaeda does not exist, nor did it continue, because of bin Laden. It will remain, evolve, and resume its actions. There is something much stronger holding them together than one man. The tremendously profitable drug trade did not exist solely because of Escobar, for example. The fact he could profit from drug addicts and the like made him an opportunist and a businessman willing to do almost anything to live the kind of life he wanted.

Both men were driven and had the resources to manifest their individual wills unto the world, but they did not exist in a vacuum. Each man was not the embodiment of evil as if each existed outside the realm of environment and context. To place the totality of blame unto each man without dissecting and unpacking the complex web of variables that created the circumstances for each to become the most wanted in the world at a certain point in time is simply irresponsible, naïve, and, quite blatantly, ignorant policy. To say they were the embodiment of evil as if they were possessed by the devil, and, thus, we or the rest of the world had nothing to do with their potential rise is quite the farce. We are embarrassing and disgracing ourselves with such reasoning. We are making a mockery out of ourselves.

Unless the policy succeeds in complete annihilation of the Other, of the enemy, of the opponent—as in complete and total genocide of bodies and the removal of discontent (control of dissemination of information) by those who remember history—then we are engaged in a potentially never-ending game. I call it a game because many celebrating in the U.S. are treating bin Laden's death as an ultimate victory of their favorite sports team. It feels like the jubilation against a rival who, after a decade of kicking our ass by going undefeated, was finally subdued to our awesomeness. This is not a game. This is not a true victory, especially if we look at the bigger picture. In our recent history, we have already heard the premature declaration of a military success as "Mission Accomplished." We have seen how accomplished that turned out in Iraq. But maybe it wasn't the accomplishment that was the problem, but the mission itself that was anemic? That's something to think about because we are heading toward a similar "mission accomplished" type of phenomenon.

Further, if we are to take such past missions and strategies— against narco-terrorism, for example—to their logical conclusions, we should also target drug consumers, not just producers/suppliers, as terrorists. George Bush, in a 1988 campaign speech, made this very clear to me, but not to himself: "The logic is simple. The cheapest way to eradicate narcotics is to destroy them at their source. [...] We need to wipe out crops wherever they are grown and take out labs wherever they exist." He took this policy to the White House, which was later implemented by succeeding presidents. Bush Sr.'s logic is quite "simple" and the "source" has been arbitrarily defined as anyone who may be responsible; anyone but the U.S. With such logic, the source is also, and primarily,

26

Unitedstatesians since they are the primary consumers. The U.S. military should then be deployed on its own territory because, as Economics 101 courses profess, the source of a business is the demand. If there is no demand, the business will most likely fail. There's a relationship, and the relationship has not found its way into counter-narcoterrorism policy to make a significant difference.

To keep Bush Sr.'s reasoning going, if we are to follow his simple logic to conclusion—a logic all succeeding presidents applied, Democrat and Republican—then why are we also not fighting the "war" on violence and the illegal arms trade within U.S. territory? Last I checked, the "source" of deaths caused by firepower is the actual gun/machine gun/bomb, etc., and the leading world supplier of arms is none other than the U.S. If we are to use the same "simple logic"—as Bush Sr. proposed and applied during the war on drugs—to justify focusing on the supplier (the "source"), then why should the U.S. not also create a policy that copies and pastes this argument against the main producer/supplier of arms?

I don't suggest we go out and enact complete genocide "at the source." What I am simply trying to illustrate is how arbitrary—and driven by self-interests—such so-called security policies have been and how ineffective they have been when they have tackled the bigger picture and larger issues. The killings of bin Laden and Escobar are variables of tactics and strategies we need to revise, reinterpret, re-evaluate, and re-envision if we are sincere about what we propose we are doing. A new discussion must arise, but it will most likely not come from the top; it may have to germinate from the bottom up. This new strategy needs to further involve (1) the place demand has in the drug aspect of the war, and (2) an understanding of the reasons—concerns and grievances—those who want to do harm to others have in the terror aspect of the war. Further, this strategy should also revise the tactics used to decrease drug production. But most importantly, we,

27

as an international community, need to have a long and honest discussion regarding the legalization of drugs. There is much more we can include on this list since I just provided a general outline, but the point is that it needs to be revised if we truly want to achieve security, progress, fruition, and a greater quality of life for all those impacted by the narco-terrorism war.

So, is it time for celebration now that bin Laden is gone? No. The issue is more complex and bigger than the man.

Not only will we "only have peace when we stop the cycle of jubilation over acts of violence," as Pamela Gerloff recently wrote, but also how can we celebrate something (especially to the extent that it has been celebrated in the U.S.) that has been proven to be ineffective, inconsistent, and counter-productive? If history has demonstrated anything with such a policy—an obsession with targeting kingpins, arbitrarily defining the "source" of the problem and what the "problem" is, and the unwillingness to recognize our own involvement in our insecurity dilemmas and how we, too, may be responsible— then I await a continuing and pro-longed narco-terrorist war; maybe under a different name and dressed in different attire in the future, but in the future nonetheless.

Hombre, It's Time to Sit down and Talk

27 September 2010, *Colombia Reports*

Since the time of La Violencia, negotiations between guerrilla groups (especially the FARC) and the government have mostly been ineffective, aside from a few successes in the early 1990s. As a result, it became fashionable for both sides to claim, "We have tried negotiations, but they haven't worked for over half a century," to justify continuing the war. The truth is that though both entities tried to negotiate, the process never really took place in good faith. This makes it difficult for negotiations to be effective. It is time for both the Santos administration and the FARC and ELN to demonstrate their sincerity through action.

In the early 1950s, when General Gustavo Rojas Pinilla was in power, he granted amnesty to both paramilitary death squads and guerrillas, and demobilization followed. However, the guerrillas never fully disarmed, and the general used violence to subdue the opposition that rose against his scrapping of agrarian reforms. Bombings, selective assassinations, and drastic displacement of the rural population resulted, and are considered by Colombian violentologists as the second phase of La Violencia. Negotiations were insincere on both sides.

In the 1980s, President Belisario Betancur negotiated a ceasefire with the FARC. This allowed the creation of a legitimate political party, Unión Patriótica (UP), to represent the concerns of the FARC, and those the guerrillas represented, on the political stage. However, the FARC never disarmed and continued "all forms of struggle." Conversely, the government did not protect the UP as promised, and, at times, even tolerated and collaborated with armed groups that targeted UP members and sympathizers for assassination. The result was the political genocide (2,000 to 5,000 dead) of the UP. The party no longer exists. Negotiations were insincere on both sides.

During the late 1990s and early 2000s, the Colombian government and the FARC attempted further negotiations. The government even demilitarized a section of Colombian territory for the FARC. However, the FARC did not disarm and used this opportunity to recruit, train, extort, kidnap, and seize a bigger role in the drug trade. Simultaneously, the government began to modernize its army, legitimized U.S. intervention under the veil of a drug war whose main purpose was really to subdue the leftist insurgency, while government-allied paramilitaries continued their pillaging and slaughter over millions of hectares of land and hundreds of thousands of lives. Negotiations were insincere on both sides.

In 2002, the people elected Álvaro Uribe Vélez to the country's highest office on the platform that since negotiations had failed, it was time for an iron fist to militarily defeat the guerrillas once and for all. The closest thing to negotiations during this eight-year period was talks of an exchange of hostages for jailed guerrillas.

To the surprise of many, President Juan Manuel Santos has demonstrated a willingness to negotiate and resolve conflicts through discourse—far more so than his predecessor. We can look at the Andean diplomatic crisis that flared up in March 2008, and which worsened in August 2009, as an example. Uribe bequeathed to President Santos one of Colombia's worst neighborly relations since the secession of Venezuela and Ecuador some 180 years ago, or of Panama in 1903, or the territorial war against Peru in the early 1930s. In less than two months in office, President Santos silenced battle drums and subdued fires of resentment, which led to a restoration of diplomatic and trade ties that seem promising for all parties involved. This is reason for optimism.

In late July, FARC leader Alfonso Cano called for talks with the new government. Santos also opened the door to negotiations. However, both sides gave different preconditions for such a step. Though I would not go as far as Vice President Angelino Garzon, who claimed on 15 September that there is no longer "reason for guerrilla groups to exist in Colombia," I will say that government preconditions for talks are reasonable: "set free all the kidnapped people without conditions, cease the practices of kidnapping, terrorism, and land mines."

If Alfonso Cano truly believes, as he claimed in February, that 70% of Colombians are in favor of a political solution to the armed conflict, then it is reasonable to accept a similar portion of the citizenry, if not a larger one, would support the government's preconditions for peace talks. It is Alfonso Cano who appears unreasonable on this point.

That is, of course, if the government is sincere and acting in good faith. History has demonstrated that it often has not during peace talks. Nevertheless, we must judge President Santos on his actions, not on the actions of previous governments. President Santos has already demonstrated his will to resolve the situations with Ecuador and Venezuela, so we know he can settle disputes peacefully.

However, I would say that if the FARC does abide by government preconditions for dialogue, the government must not use this as an opportunity to ambush the guerrillas or civilians, nor should it tolerate or support other illegally armed groups doing so. For peace talks to be successful, sincere, and in good faith, this does not seem absurd.

Let's begin by abandoning the discourse of trying to figure out who threw the first stone during the past 60-plus years, to justify the violence used by one party against another. Both parties have done horrendous things and are guilty of extreme human rights violations and crimes against humanity. I see this as an opportune time for a political solution to the armed conflict. Though I am skeptical about how much each party is willing to concede during negotiations—if preconditions are met and they sit down for a chat—I hope my skepticism is proven ill-founded.

Colombia's Historical Lack of Hegemony and Institutionalized Violence

April 2013

Introduction

In Colombia, an effective modern nation-state has never existed, highly due to the country's historical lack of hegemony and institutionalized violence. It is important to curb the traditional might-makes-right method of conflict resolution and that the Colombian state gain legitimacy if the country is ever to realize its potential, because prolonged war drains the country's most essential resources and creates an aggressively vengeful environment of resentment and resistance. I have organized the essay into the following two sections:

- **The Power Vacuum.** In the first section, I tackle the power vacuum created by liberation from colonial

Spain and the roots of the interparty violence that ensued while those in power tried to best organize the new republic—from before liberation from Spain to the Thousand Days' War, 1899-1902.

- **The Birth of Class Consciousness in the 20th Century.** In the second section, I address how the 20th century brought forth new threats, both foreign and domestic, to the two political parties, which tried desperately and aggressively to hold on to the traditional system of oligarchic, plutocratic, and kratocractic power—from the end of the Thousand Days' War to the end of the Cold War. Amid a perpetual state of infrastructural weakness and a fragmented sovereignty, Northern imperialism, the communist threat, and the global illicit drug trade added new elements to the already complex and bloody history of a country still, after nearly two centuries, trying to learn how to coexist in a plural world.

I. The Power Vacuum

Fragmented sovereignty

> *To extricate our nascent republic from this chaos, not even the full weight of our moral faculties will suffice unless we can learn to unify our country: its governmental structure, its legislative body, and its national spirit. Unity, unity, unity— that must be our motto. If the blood of our citizens is diverse, let us make it one. If our constitution has divided the powers, let us unify them. If our laws are moribund relics of every ancient and modern despotism, let us tear down this monstrous edifice and, obliterating even its ruins, build a temple of justice in whose sacred precincts we can dictate a ... code of law.*
>
> Simón Bolívar[1]

Though one can find almost unanimous support for the claim that Colombia is a fragmented sovereignty—many of whom assert, like James Rochlin, that there exists an irregular pattern of violence and a sense of space that has exacerbated political fragmentation that is feudal in character[2]—there is less consensus on the causes of political violence. For example, there have been those—like Bert Ruiz,[3] Charles Bergquist,[4] and Jenny Pearce[5]—who have argued for the primary causes of political violence as directly tied to the unequal distribution of wealth, violent and non-violent oppression at the hands of the government, and political exclusion of individuals and groups traditionally Othered in Colombia (such as, Amerindians, Afro-Colombians, peasants, women, the poor, and the lower classes). Other explanations have come from those in the economic conflict theory camp, such as Paul Collier, who identify the armed conflict as one of economic greed. This perspective leads many of this school to stress the importance of certain legal and illicit industries as the root causes of political violence in Colombia. The illegal arms trade, the cocaine trade, and "wildcat mining," for example, help provide illegal armed groups—such as neo-paramilitary organizations, guerrillas, and criminal bands—with funds to maintain their operations, satisfy their economic aspirations, and increase their positioning in the struggle for power and authority.

Though all these explanations—along with others, such as neorealist, neoliberal, biological, psychological, religious, epistemological, and sociological ones—have something important to contribute to the discourse, and though there are kernels of truths to all these explanations, it is in institutional analysis where I find a more cohesive and holistic explanation for the primary cause of political violence in Colombia. Perpetual state infrastructural weakness has been at the root of Colombia's historical lack of hegemony and its institutionalized bellicose culture.[6] In conjunction with the usual explanations, it is the fragmented nation-state—feudal and fractured by its demanding terrain—that has set the parameters for the power struggle that has shaped the country's armed conflict. As Alex McDougall pointed out, "The absence of a strong state presence, combined with the

35

availability of lootable resources explains and predicts the patterns of rebel consolidation in Colombia." It is precisely these "patterns of historical state weakness" that help explain "how Colombia's three major armed groups[7] have formed, developed, and mounted continual challenges to the sovereignty and territorial integrity of the Colombian state."[8] Add to this scenario the fact that Colombia has one of the most difficult terrains[9] in Latin America and the goal of unity becomes extremely complicated.

It is, however, a challenging endeavor to fully assert blame in Colombia's armed conflict since the conditions on the ground have largely allowed and called for such fragmentation and political violence to evolve. Becoming a modern nation-state after having been a colony has never been an easy enterprise. After a bloody decade that resulted in liberation from the chains of Spanish colonialism, the founders and the people of the new Colombian Republic—then called Gran Colombia— were presented with the most difficult task for any transitioning former colony: how to best organize themselves. It was one thing to want a governing system quite like the one with which the young United States (U.S.) at the time was experimenting; it was quite another undertaking to take that castle from the sky and build it on earth.

Struggle: liberation and transition

We can attribute part of the success against Spain to Simón Bolívar's analysis of concrete reality and the facts on the ground as basis for action, and not mere abstract principles. He looked for the spirit of the laws for the country for which they were to be written. Though he praised the then recently founded federalist system in the U.S. as being at that moment the "most perfect and most suitable for guaranteeing human happiness in society," he also recognized that his own citizens were not yet ready for such a system because "it requires political virtues and skills far superior to ours." Bolívar understood the importance of adjusting actions to circumstance, "to the context of the times, [humans], and circumstances in which it operates."[10] In turn, when it came time to construct national constitutions for the liberated countries in the Northern Andes region of Latin America, he suggested not striving for the most ideologically perfect system of government, "but for the most likely of attainment."[11]

He interpreted the historicity of his territory and people and concluded it would be impractical to persevere in the direction of the U.S. federalist system and England's monarchical combination of democracy and aristocracy. Though both countries were experiencing much fortune and splendor, to strive for what they had, in the same manner, was beyond the capacity of Latin America at the time.[12] Though he suggested it was good to study these systems of government, it was not in their best interest to imitate them. He advised never to forget that "the existence of a government depends not on its political theory, or its form, or its administrative mechanism, but on its appropriateness to the nature and character of the nation for which it is instituted."[13] Similarly, he concluded that a country's constitution should be reformed if the moral climate of its people called for it.[14]

He found the essence of government to reside not in principles, but in humans and their historical situation.[15] "Bear in mind, Legislators," Bolívar stated, "that nations are made up of cities and villages, and that the happiness of the state depends on their well-being."[16] Through sentiments, such as, "Give us a government where the law is obeyed, where the judge is respected, where the people are free, a government that forbids any transgression against the popular will, against the mandate of the people,"[17] it is clear he determined unity gave rise to and preserved order.[18] Here, he further recognized that the stability of a state required a balance between consent and coercion, "a national resolve aimed equally and consistently at two goals: the moderation of the general will and the curtailment of public authority."[19] There is much debate as to whether or not Bolívar himself followed his own words. His push for a centralized government and flirtation with life-term high political offices made many citizens and fellow politicians interpret his actions as too authoritarian for a democracy. Nevertheless, though his actions may be controversial, his words are wise. We can still apply many of his assessments and aspirations to today's situation. Fundamentally, an effective state can only arise if there is unity, legitimacy, a marriage between coercion and consent, and a construction of policy based on conditions on the ground and not some kind of absolute and universal principle that is supposed to work for all peoples always regardless of their own complex and unique contexts and histories.

In retrospect, winning the war of liberation against Spain was easier than uniting the country, let alone the region. Though he was very much a pragmatic individual in many respects, Bolívar's aspiration for creating a unified Latin America in the 19th century was quite an ambitious, yet naïve, goal once we consider the limitations carved out by self-interests, terrain, white supremacy, misogyny, religion, communication technologies, and transport mechanisms of the time. The dream of a unified region is more feasible today than it was two-hundred years ago, but still tremendously difficult, as Colombia is testament.

Crisis of authority and bad inheritance

A state cannot address the obstacles I discussed unless it is effective. However, the question of cause and effect often surfaces. In Colombia, the initial inadequate transition from colonialism to a nation-state, and the inability of legislators to construct formidable power-sharing mechanisms and to fill the political, economic, and other vacuums left behind by Spain's departure, caused disorder. Thereafter, that disorder produced more weakness in the state where it became difficult to pinpoint what was a cause and what was the effect, since most of the time the variables were intertwined by being both simultaneously. That said, I claim one initial cause was the country's inability to fill the voids, which is no easy task for any former colony.

Further, unlike its neighbor Brazil, Colombia did not inherit institutions, epistemology, modernity, and peaceful conflict resolution mechanisms from its former colonial power. Brazil was able to enjoy greater prosperity than Spain's Latin American colonies upon gaining independence because the Portuguese monarch, Dom João, moved to Brazil to avoid being captured by Napoleon's armies when they invaded Portugal. When the monarch moved to Brazil, he made Rio de Janeiro the capital of the Portuguese empire and ended Brazil's colonial status by proclaiming the country a coequal kingdom with the same rank as Portugal. As a result, Brazil enjoyed a much greater level of prosperity than any of Spain's Latin American colonies, which included inheriting many of Portugal's institutions. For example, the printing press came to Brazil along with academies and universities, as well as the founding of the Bank of Brazil. These institutions remained in place after Brazil's independence and provided the country with a working structure of government that allowed it to avoid the destruction of war suffered by Spain's Latin American colonies, and to emerge as a prosperous independent country. Colombia suffered greatly from its bloody transition into democracy in comparison to Brazil, who had a relatively bloodless transition. Unlike Brazil, Colombia, even after independence, remained largely epistemologically in pre-modernity, choosing to organize itself predominantly in feudal city-states while simultaneously inheriting the debilitating costs of prolonged war—casualties, broken families, debt, loss of labor, resentment, and the overwhelming memory of having to resolve conflicts by means of force and coercion.

Colombia was not so fortunate as its neighbor in this manner, as laws became discredited and no longer represented the will of the people.[20] Post-independence, the only ones Bolívar could blame were his own compatriots for their inability to unify civil and political society to create a grandiose state.[21] This inability Bolívar considered "the mortal poison that pushed the country into her grave."[22] Public order was a fantasy because no general laws existed and those that did exist were ineffectively enforced and regulated, which was to ultimately lead the country into a "state of confusion."[23] The crisis drove Bolívar to write that human rights under the yoke of Spain were actually more respected than the immediate decades thereafter. Bolívar acknowledged there was no good faith, and that "treaties [were] scraps of paper, […] constitutions empty texts, […] elections pitched battles, […] freedom mere anarchy, and […] lives pure torture." The situation got so dreadful that Bolívar thought that if things could not change, the people "would be better off dead." He assessed there were no longer any guarantees for freedom and security, and all that remained were hopes and fantasies for a better tomorrow or a desire to return to how things used to be, even if under the tutelage of Spain.[24] Through this experience he deduced there was "no power more difficult to maintain than that of a new prince."[25]

A large detriment to the birth of the nation was its inability and lack of desire to fulfil promises made to the lower classes and undervalued peoples during the revolutionary war. First, élites, Bolívar among them, only sought to include the indigenous, the slaves, and the peasants in the revolution (like the *llaneros*, without whom liberation would have been almost impossible) *after* the élite had been militarily defeated by the Spaniards during that first half decade of fighting during the 1810s. This meant the Spanish American élite needed soldiers and support from the people to win. If the élite could have secured liberation without the people, they would have, which is exactly what they tried to do initially.[26] Second, the promises the élite made to those originally overlooked for unity during the first years of war did not fully materialize. Once the bourgeoisie attained control, the whip was transferred from the Spaniards to the Colombian élite.

Such a situation occurred throughout the region post-liberation. "Culturally, independent Spanish America," Carlos Fuentes described in *The Buried Mirror*, "turned its back on both its Indian and black heritages, judging them to be barbarous."[27] It became quite clear that to fill the political and cultural vacuum the élites in Colombia regarded the Other as expendable. Though Spain was no longer in power, the conquest was not over. Now it was the very own Spanish Americans who were the conquistadors "acting exactly like descendants of Cortés and Pizarro. Only the uniforms had changed."[28] This notion excluded the will, heart, and mind of the very people for whom independence supposedly took place. Consequently, Colombia's history is underlined by the élite taking wealth and power from the people. For many, the war of liberation was just one group of élites against another group of élites fighting for control of land and human resources. As Fuentes wrote, "Like the Crown before them, the new republics seemed remote from the everyday concerns of the workers and peasants, and of the landowners and local political bosses, who wished to enhance their power and privileges, not hand them over to their laborers."[29] The stage was set for the ever-growing conflict between what evolved into the two predominant Colombian political parties—Conservatives and Liberals—and the class struggle and the wars on drugs and terror that were to come in the latter half of the 20th century.

The how-should-we-organize-ourselves debate also set the stage for a Colombian form of conflict resolution: might-makes-right. Though known as the second oldest democracy in the hemisphere and the longest history of free elections in Latin America, the goal of each party has been to subdue the opposition if elected. Surprisingly, unlike regional neighbors, Colombian dictators have only seized control three times: twice during the 19th century (which lasted less than a year each before civilian rule was restored), and once in the 20th century for five years. All three cases, shockingly, were largely supported by *el pueblo*. History illustrates how Colombians are inclined to violent forms of conflict resolution. Though in comparison to the rest of Latin America Colombia has no real history of violent dictatorships, this should not over-shadow the fact that Colombian institutions and the people themselves consent to using force and coercion as the predominant, systemic, and widespread means for securing interests. This has led to a dominant culture of violence accepted as an unfortunate reality—as if it were natural phenomenon for which the people must brace themselves; as if violence was an inherent genetic trait to Colombians and, thus, the question has not been whether violence would be an effective form of negotiation and reconciliation, but, instead, how much violence is needed to suppress others into obedience. Not much has changed in 21ˢᵗ-century Colombia since one of the main reasons for the current armed conflict regards access and control of resources, both human and natural.[30] If Bolívar were alive today, he may not be surprised to see that the lack of hegemony in Colombia is as important an issue as it was two centuries ago.

Roots of 19th-century interparty warfare

Historian Catherine C. LeGrand summarized the 1800s as a bloody century between Liberals and Conservatives whose disagreements led to 33 total years of civil war, thereby giving rise to 64 differently sized revolutions and 11 constitution changes.[31] The century was politically chaotic, even by Latin American standards. The consequences of this organized chaos—organized because it was guided by a framework and certain rules by which both political parties seemed to agree to follow—devastated the country. Political violence not only left over a quarter of a million individuals dead during the century, but the material destruction could also be measured in years' worth of economic output. For example, during the start of the final civil war of the century, the Colombian peso was four to one against the U.S. dollar. However, after the war, it was one hundred to one; in turn paralyzing the Colombian economy in some regions for four years.[32] By the end of 1903, four percent of the male population was lost because of the great civil war.

These prolonged and incessant internal wars completely exhausted the country and created long-lasting feuds, fed the fires of anger and resentment, fragmented families and communities, and helped create a polarized environment where the conflict between the citizenry looked more like a religious war than a political clash. Even before the two major political parties were formally established in the late 1840s, the country was in violent turmoil.

The early 19th century is quite an important period in that it set the tone for the instability that was to follow for the rest of the century. This long period of volatility and insecurity, even before the war of independence, was the foundation for the ever-growing conflict between what evolved into the two predominant Colombian political parties: Conservatives and Liberals. The Conservatives were followers of Bolívar, while the Liberals fell in line with the opinions of Bolívar's second in command, Francisco de Paula Santander. The Conservatives supported a highly centralized government with strong ties to the Roman Catholic Church. The Liberals supported the separation of church and state[33] and a decentralized federalist government like that of the U.S. These tensions escalated from the initial broken ties between Bolívar and Santander in 1825.

Between 1796 and 1806, the centralists and federalists engaged in constant fighting. This resulted in provinces and some cities where regional élites established separate autonomous juntas. The fragmented sovereignty of Colombia started before the war of liberation had even begun whereby these juntas proclaimed their own distinct sovereignty and autonomy from the others. Bolívar's dream of unification of the Americas was just that: a pipedream. Realities on the ground suggested this dream would almost certainly fail from the start unless force was used to attain it. In fact, the continuation of long-standing conflict before the war of liberation was the main cause that led to the secession of Ecuador and Venezuela in 1830 from Gran Colombia.[34]

The question regarding how best to organize the new republic was a debate that continued long after the war against Spain for liberation. Every single civil war during the century was rooted in whether Colombia should follow in the footsteps of the U.S. and become a federation or if it should create a highly centralized state with the Catholic Church as its moral compass. The costliest of these civil wars was the Thousand Days' War, which marked not only the turn of the century but also forced leaders from the Left and the Right to deliberate and construct new power-sharing mechanisms to avoid another violent century of prolonged war. Nevertheless, before the Liberals and Conservatives constituted this new power-sharing mechanism, democracy in Colombia meant majority ruled. The party that got elected tried to change the system to serve only its own interests, thereby neglecting the concerns and grievances of the opposition while simultaneously using force to subdue it. The opposition, meanwhile, would look for ways to take power, also mostly by means of coercive measures.

Though Colombia practiced democracy, the electoral system was largely to blame for the political violence throughout the century. As Sebastián Mazzuca and James A. Robinson argued, there was a causal relationship, not a coincidental relationship, between the violence of the 19th century and the relative peace of the early 20th century:

> Before 1905, institutions favoring power monopolization by a single party forced the opposition into revolutionary tactics and the government into violent repression, whereas starting in 1905, the emergence of institutions ensuring both parties a share of political power roughly proportional to their electoral force allowed for a peaceful interaction between government and opposition. From the standpoint of power-sharing mechanisms, the key institutional change

44

was the replacement in 1905 of majoritarian rule by the
incomplete vote, a special kind of electoral system.
Colombia in turn switched from the incomplete vote to
proportional representation in 1929.[35]

With the lack of conflict resolution institutions in the 19th
century, the kind of democracy Colombians had constructed
for themselves allowed for such interparty warfare to evolve.
During this period, the Liberal Party and the Conservative
Party were simultaneously political and military organizations,
wherein the key circumstance that allowed either party to gain
access and keep control of the government was armed
advantage.

The majoritarian electoral system of the 19th century was
detrimental for conflict resolution. Colombian majoritarian
rule

introduce[d] a distortion between level of popular
support and institutional power: for the winner of the
electoral context, [the majoritarian system] amplif[ied] in
congress its popular power, and [the majoritarian
system] weaken[ed] (or even nullif[ied]) that of the rest
of the parties.[36]

In light of this, there is a lot of truth to what Bonaficio Vélez
attributed to be some of the major causes of civil wars in
Colombia during its first one-hundred years: "[M]ost of our
civil wars [...] have originated in the lack of properly
representative governments, in the systematic and hateful
exclusion that was installed in the republic. Minority
representation prevents revolutionary attempts."[37]

The Radical Olympus and the Regeneration

Two of the major distinct eras where this was most evident
were during the Olimpo Radical (Radical Olympus) and the
Hegemonía Conservadora (Conservative Hegemony). The
Radical Olympus took place from 1860 through the mid-
1880s. During this period, Liberals took it upon themselves to
drastically reform government institutions to favor their one-

sided political preference. Their goal during this time was to fully remove the country from its colonial past. It was under the Radical Olympus that the hemisphere saw the most extreme version of federalism, and between 1863 through 1886 the Liberals changed the country's name and officially became the United States of Colombia. This new U.S. sought to completely remove or limit the cultural and institutional powers of the Catholic Church by, among other things, expropriating the Church's wealth and transferring it to country's industrialists, removing the Church's role in the system of education, and forced the Jesuit order out of the country. Up to this point, Colombian institutions had been centralized under the rule of the Conservatives, and the Liberals looked to change this by giving more autonomy to the states. This all-out attack on the Catholic Church and Conservative ideals led to substantial periods of the government preparing its military apparatus for repressing the opposition. It also led the Conservatives to create their own private armies to try to take down the government and defend themselves against the government's usage of its military power. This hard-lined Liberal stance provoked a violent reaction by the Conservatives, especially from the religious sectors of the country.

The tactics used by the Conservatives during the Conservative Hegemony from 1885 through 1900, a period deemed La Regeneración (The Regeneration), were similar as those used by Liberals during their Radical Olympus. The major difference was the goal guiding the party. The Conservatives used their new capacity to create the kind of government they pleased. Both periods of coercive dominance were marked by one party imposing its will and policies over the other. Once the Conservatives retook power—and after crushing a Liberal Revolution that tried to regain power after it had lost the elections—the Conservatives made significant changes to institutions. They introduced a new constitution that officially ended the country's federalist experiment and became a very

centralized republic, officially changing its name from the
United States of Colombia to the Republic of Colombia. This
new centralist constitution remained in place, though amended
many times, until 1991. With the Conservatives now in power,
they looked to reintroduce the role of the Catholic Church in
education, politics, economics, and other cultural institutions.
The states, now recognized as departments, lost the political
autonomy they had gained under Liberal rule. With this new
transition into a centralized republic, the president gained
extraordinary powers and the Conservatives granted the
government the ability to more heavily intervene in the
economy, which was decentralized and ruled by free-market
principles during the Radical Olympus. Most government
spending was allocated by the Conservatives to contain and
militarily repress opposition movements.[38] The Liberals did
not take this new political hegemony lying down. The Liberals
were constantly preparing for revolution—at times even going
to neighboring countries for "diplomatic missions" to attain
arms. Nevertheless, the two main revolutions against the
Conservative Hegemony—1895 and the Thousand Days'
War—were unsuccessful, just like the 1876-1877 war against
the Radical Olympus was a failed undertaking by the
Conservatives.

It was this reactionary turn to the Right—the Conservatives'
policy changes and near monopoly over government
institutions since the mid-1880s—that set the Liberals on a
course to radically counter these new measures by trying to
forcefully retake power in 1899. After the Conservatives
rejected the Liberals' political pleas for proper representation
in the government, war ensued. The predictive words of
Liberal Rafael Uribe Uribe in September of 1898, just before
the war, entirely capture the sentiment:

> I am not threatening or provoking. I am not coming here
> as the Roman consul before the Senate of Carthage,
> bringing in his uniform the options 'war or peace' for
> you to choose. I am just predicting the unavoidable. I am

> just warning that this, which today is a peaceful petition in favor of our rights, if you deny it, tomorrow will become a demand backed by the arms, and then, after costly sacrifices, one of two things will occur: if we win, we will give to ourselves not only what we are demanding today, or the full rights that belong to us, but even more than that, at your expense, because of the irresistible impetus given by victory; or, if we lose, not for that will our right die, and you will spend more resources in continuing oppressing us than those required to live with us in peace and equality…. Give us the freedom to make public and defend our rights with the vote, the quill, and the lips; otherwise, nobody in the world will have enough power to silence the barrels of our rifles.[39]

Originally, it was thought this new civil war would not last more than a few months, but, instead, persisted for a few years and became known as the Thousand Days' War, which left the country in the worst shape it was ever in since liberation from Spain. Two important outcomes of the last civil war of the 19th century were that it forced the two parties to (i) negotiate a new power-sharing system that helped prevent factions from violently uprising and (ii) it led to the institutionalization of the military and its separation from party politics.

Politicians construct a new power-sharing mechanism from the ruins of the 19th century

Preventing future domestic and international wars became a top priority, especially after the Thousand Days' War and the loss of Panama in 1903. The new power-sharing mechanisms that surfaced after the war may be considered an anomaly by neorealists who assume that violent force is the most important factor in political relations. The history of Colombia's oligarchy and élite is quite bellicose and has given rise to equally violent opposition movements. Nevertheless, not all Colombian history is one of wars and armed conflict. The country's Conservative leaders in the early 1900s negotiated peace with the extremely politically weak and recently militarily defeated Liberals—concessions that brought

48

forth decades of peace after experiencing an entire century of non-stop political violence. This raises the following important questions:[40] Why order in the early 20th century after the chaos of the 19th century? Why did Conservatives negotiate, reform, and accept a reduction of their power? Opening our eyes to potential answers to these questions may serve our current armed conflict situation well.

The Conservatives saw political power-sharing, brought forth in this case by electoral reform, as a means to achieve political pacification of their Liberal opposition. The strategic concession the Conservatives made to the Liberals is extremely noteworthy considering they had just (i) absolutely crushed the Liberals during the Thousand Days' War and (ii) the Conservatives had a near monopoly over government institutions since the mid-1880s. For example, Liberals held merely two legislative seats between 1886 and the end of the war. After a war-torn century grounded on might-makes-right policies by both Liberals and Conservatives depending on who was at the head of government. Exemplified by the Radical Olympus and the Conservative Hegemony, both parties, weak and strong, recognized that the Colombian brand of the might-makes-right strategy was ineffective for securing national interests because when violence was accepted as both means *and* end it could only lead to more violence, which would yield a weak and fragmented sovereignty. Their evidence was the 19th century.

As highlighted by Sebastian Mazzuca and James A. Robinson, during the political debates immediately before and after the Thousand Days' War, Liberals suggested that power and violence were actually opposites,[41] not the same or complementary, and, thus, the conventional ordering of things in Colombia needed to be ruptured and replaced by the real power inherent in power-sharing mechanisms between weak and strong. Political exclusion of minority and militarily weakened groups had to stop. Concessions by Conservatives allowed for the manifestation of their interests and security without constant fear of harm, revolt, conspiracy, coups, or subjugation to Liberals—as had happened previously during the Radical Olympus—if Conservatives lost their military and political dominance. They recognized that if they continued with their traditional might-makes-right policy after the great war, that it would only produce more enemies against the Conservatives and inspire prolonged armed opposition.

It was not until this new power-sharing mechanism was in place, which allowed Liberals more representation in government,[42] that the state was in a more effective position than before to consider dealing with other pressing obstacles. Once both parties were unified—or, at least content with how power would be disseminated and shared—the state was able to work toward acquiring a monopoly of force. The previous century was marked by wars led mostly by men who were not trained in military tactics or strategy. These strongmen were civilian caudillos and lawyers turned generals. Unfortunately, the result was an increased amount of blood spilled and intensification of the violent conflicts, which created a vulnerable state. It was not until the early 20th century that the country finally decided to establish formal, professionally trained armed forces. Fearing prolonged internal strife, the two political parties negotiated a new power-sharing mechanism that would, ideally, prevent factions from violently opposing the elected government.

II. The Birth of Class Consciousness in the 20th Century

The second phase of the Conservative Hegemony

There was also a fear that a threat could come from outside Colombia's borders. By the end of 1903, immediately following the Thousand Days' War, seven percent of the country's territory was lost. The U.S. took advantage of the fact that the war left the country in shambles as it poorly positioned Colombia. Colombia was so weak that all the U.S. had to do was show up to Panamanian shores with its navy. Colombia did not make a great effort to fight. It knew it could not keep Panama from seceding if the U.S. was going to militarily intervene. Without having to fire a shot, the U.S. got what it wanted from Colombia: the contract to construct and have full control of the Panama Canal.[43] For the previous four decades the U.S. negotiated with Colombia to do so, but the U.S. demanded too much, and, as a result, Colombia did not want to give the contract to the North Americans. Consequently, since the succeeding administrations in Washington, D.C., could not get their hands on the canal via cooperation, the North Americans decided to flex their muscles. As Theodore Roosevelt explained, "I took the Canal Zone and let Congress debate, and while the debate goes on, the canal does also."[44] The price, apparently, for this theft of Colombian land during the period of Roosevelt's invention of Panama was worth 25 million U.S. dollars—this is how much the U.S. paid to Colombia in the 1920s for reparations.[45] U.S. disposition at the time put Colombia on alert since Roosevelt was quite ready to use his big stick diplomacy if he felt U.S. interests threatened: "Chronic wrongdoing [...] in the Western Hemisphere [...] may force the United States [...] to the exercise of an international police power."

Because of the Thousand Days' War and the loss of Panama, Colombian authoritarian President Rafael Reyes, 1903-1909, was wise enough to acknowledge the importance of establishing formally trained armed forces. In 1907, Colombia contracted Chile to instruct and prepare Colombia for its first official and unified army. The Colombian government even established a military college at the capital. Nevertheless, with the overthrow of Reyes, the country lost interest in creating an army officer class. Colombia made little progress toward developing the country's armed forces until after Colombia engaged in the 1932 to 1933 war against Peru over the territory of Leticia, located at the southern tip of the Colombian Amazon. After opponents overthrew Reyes and before the war with Peru, the government used the Colombian military apparatus mostly for civilian projects, such as building roads. In fact, many ministers during the 1920s thought the army was not worth maintaining. They did not attach the notion of national security with having a strong army, as did Reyes. By the time the war started, even though the number of troops went from 139 officers and 1,500 enlisted men in 1922 to 6,000 in 1932, Colombia's military was proportionally the smallest in the entire hemisphere. Peru, for example, had more than twice the budget for military affairs and more than twice the number of troops as Colombia.

The war against Peru was a humiliating affair and awakened the country to the sorry state of its armed forces. The war resulted in an increased interest in developing the country's military. The military budget expenditure grew quickly and quite drastically, especially when Colombia became an ally of the U.S. during World War Two. To put it into perspective, what follows is the country's annual military budget in Colombian pesos from 1932 through 1945: four million at the start of the war against Peru, eight million immediately after the war, almost 16 million by 1943 and nearly 25 million by the end of 1945.

Though the war against Peru was shameful, it was another event during this time that gave workers and peasants a glimpse of the class and production conflict that was to come in later decades. Toward the end of 1928, an event in Colombia known as the *masacre de las bananeras* took place. The banana massacre occurred in a town near Santa Marta after a month-long strike by United Fruit Company workers who demanded better working conditions.[46] The government sent in a military regiment to subdue those identified as subversives. The strike was the largest labor movement the country had ever seen. Though it is debated as to whether the military was sent at the request of the United Fruit Company, the U.S., or the Colombian government, and whether the body count was between nine or 2,000 dead as a result, one thing is clear: Colombian security forces took up arms against its citizens to protect the interests of the United Fruit Company and the U.S. A series of official U.S. telegrams and dispatches during the strike expressed that the Colombian government had given the U.S. Bogotá Embassy the guarantee that U.S. interests would be secured:

> [T]hrough Minister of Foreign Affairs who on Saturday told me government would send additional troops and would arrest all strike leaders and transport them to prison at Cartagena; that government would give adequate protection to American interests involved [...][47]

> Situation outside Santa Marta City unquestionably very serious: outside zone is in revolt; military who have orders 'not to spare ammunition' have already killed and wounded about fifty strikers. [Colombian] Government now talks of general offensive against strikers [...][48]

> The Legation at Bogotá reports that categorical orders have been given to the authorities at Santa Marta to protect all American interests [...][49]

Fearing that Colombian force would not be enough to deal with the "Communists" and to secure U.S. interests, the U.S. requested to send their own troops.

> Feeling against the [Colombian] Government by the proletariat which is shared by some of the soldiers is high and it is doubtful if we can depend upon the Colombian Government for protection. May I respectfully suggest that my request for the presence within calling distance of an American war ship be granted [...][50]

> Troop train from banana zone just arrived in Santa Marta with all American citizens. No Americans killed or wounded. Guerrilla warfare now continuing in the zone but military forces are actively engaged in clearing the district of the Communists [...][51]

> I have the honor to report that the Bogotá representative
> of the United Fruit Company told me yesterday that the
> total number of strikers killed by the Colombian military
> exceeded one thousand [...] while the number of soldiers
> killed was one [...][52]

The Banana Massacre of 1928 is considered one of the roots
of and justifications for leftist guerrillas in the country, as the
workers and peasants tried to secure improved working
conditions, agrarian reform, political voice in government, and
to protect themselves from U.S.-supported force and terror
used by the Colombian state against its own people.

Flirting with modernity and class consciousness

By 1930, the political climate had changed and a new period,
regarded as the Liberal Republic, began. We can remember the
era between 1930 and 1946 for something essential to the
organization of the Colombian state. The end of the
Conservative Hegemony in 1930 unleashed numerous
reforms, some not seen since the days of the Radical Olympus.
The series of Liberal Party administrations during this sixteen-
year period pushed through land reforms that infuriated the
Conservatives. Furthermore, the Liberal Party, with its
initiatives of trying to modernize the country—a time of
industrialization and urbanization not previously seen in
Colombia—challenged traditional conservative mores and
values. When the Liberal Republic fell in 1946 because of a
divided Liberal party, the new Conservative government used
coercive methods to regain the land it lost after 1930.

After the end of World War Two, the U.S. increased its role in
Colombian domestic affairs. During the middle of the 20th
century, U.S. security policy focused more heavily on the
communist threat, which had grown significantly since the days
of the Banana Massacre. U.S. role in Colombian security policy
grew directly with its containment policy during the Cold War
and Alliance for Progress program in the 1960s, which was
designed to generate economic cooperation between Americas

North and South. It was during this decade that U.S. intervention in Colombia helped solidify a guerrilla movement. However, before I unpack the violence of the 1960s, I must address the period of Colombia's history called La Violencia (The Violence) to set the proper foundation.

La Violencia (roughly between 1948 and 1958) is considered to have been sparked by El Bogotázo. El Bogotázo is regarded as the greatest urban riot in the history of Latin America, which spontaneously erupted after populist Colombian Congressman Jorge Eliécer Gaitán—at the time a presidential candidate fighting for workers' rights and critical of his government for favoring U.S. interests over those of Colombians'—was assassinated on 9 April 1948.[53] During the period of La Violencia, as historian Herbert Braun expressed, Liberals went around killing Conservatives, Conservatives went around killing Liberals,

> [t]he fighting out in the countryside seemed so senseless, so difficult to comprehend, that few Colombians to this day really have a feeling that they know what happened, and historians still don't quite know what to say about it.[54]

It was throughout the course of this violent decade that peasants and laborers for the first time in the country's history really came to understand their own class consciousness.

Before this period, all civil wars were between Liberals and Conservatives. Battle lines were drawn not based on ethnicity, level of education, wealth, or class, but on whether one was Liberal or Conservative, which, like a religion, a person was born into. Peasants tending to the lands of Conservative caudillos aligned themselves politically with their landowning masters. The same thing went for the peasants of Liberal landowners. Some regions of the country were known for their political slants. These sentiments were passed down from generation to generation and were helped by the fact that the country was highly regionalized, feudal in nature, and organized into what could be recognized as small city-states within the country itself. The difficult terrain fragmented the country and made not only physical movement difficult, but also what often comes with migration: the introduction of new ideas. The many policy changes of the Liberal Republic between 1930 and 1946, which attempted to modernize the country for the first time, greatly shook up traditional forms of organization. With industrialization came urbanization, and with urbanization peasants and laborers, both Liberal and Conservative, from different regions for the first time really started to intermix. This new internal migration helped the Liberal poor and the Conservative poor for the first time see how much they had in common and how much the peasantry and laborers really differed from the traditional oligarchs. Though the reforms and initiatives during the Liberal Republic may have planted the seeds for the poor to potentially recognize their class consciousness, it was not until the Conservative government took power in 1946 that such seeds began to flourish—its full embrace not entirely coming until the second half of La Violencia.

The political violence enacted by the new Conservative government gave rise to Liberal uprisings the administration tried to subdue. As a result, the government armed Conservative peasants all over the country, who also received support from the national police. Essentially, the Conservative government created paramilitary death squads. Police officers who were members of the Liberal Party were also dismissed, fully demarcating this new civil war between political affiliations. To counter the Conservative government's move, the Liberal Party armed the Liberal peasantry. With further help from some in the Communist Party, the movement against the government was able to produce a counter-army of over 10,000, by some estimates. These insurgents stretched throughout the country and would later on form small guerrilla groups.

Though the first phase of La Violencia started similarly as other armed internal conflicts where the élites fought for institutional dominance and Liberals and Conservatives, regardless of class, fought out the battles, it was not until the second phase of La Violencia that class consciousness arrived and the old forms of alignment during violent conflict slowly ceased to exist. Nevertheless, the fighting morphed and continued. As a result, after a decade of cruel and atrocious violence, massacres, and torture, the wake of the violence left around 300,000 dead. In a sad turn of events, the Conservative Party created a self-fulfilling prophecy. The government used political violence to try to reshape the country into how it was before industrialization and urbanization—modernity—began to challenge traditional conservative values. However, it was the political violence itself—large-scale displacements of populations throughout the country and systematic military operations enacted against those who called for agrarian reform—that helped solidify the class consciousness of the lower classes. If the poor did not already have class consciousness by the beginning of La Violencia, they did by the time the 1960s arrived.

La Violencia, the National Front, and containing the communist threat

This circumstance of La Violencia led to two unusual cases in Latin American political history. The first was the 1953 coup d'état backed by *both* Liberals *and* Conservatives. La Violencia left the country so exhausted that the main political parties decided a dictator, in the form of General Gustavo Rojas Pinilla, was the only way to secure peace and stability. The second came in 1957 and 1958 when the country formed a military junta as a transition into a deal between the Liberals and Conservatives to share political control through an agreement known as the Frente Nacional (National Front). The Liberals and Conservatives alternated the presidency every four years, and the Congress was balanced by one half Liberals and the other half Conservative representatives.

In 1953, Rojas gave amnesty to leftist guerrillas and right-wing death squads, and demobilization occurred. Some guerrillas, however, conserved their arms in secret. During 1955, the second phase of La Violencia commenced, sparked by Rojas getting rid of agrarian reforms and taking aggressive action to silence opposition. The Colombian army took drastic measures (e.g., bombing) that impacted civilians and non-combatants. These acts displaced a significant number of the rural population. Those displaced took refuge in the areas under the control of the guerrilla. The actions by Rojas during this time created a stronger feeling in certain peasant sectors that only the guerrilla could guarantee protection against élite leaders and politicians who rejected any idea of agrarian reform. Élite leaders and politicians used force and coercion to ensure those who called for agrarian reform were subdued.[55] As a consequence, the exclusion of much of the Colombian population occurred since only two parties were allowed under the National Front: Liberal and Conservative. The new government alliance identified all other parties as illegitimate. These two parties were both capitalist in nature and only really differed in the role religion should play in politics, and whether the government should be centralized.

The National Front introduced a counter-insurgency security policy, supported by Washington, that almost completely disregarded the grievances of those mostly impacted by the violence of the 1940s and '50s. Instead of implementing different strategies for short-term and long-term problems in Colombian violence—which could have included political, social, economic, and military foundations—what transpired was a security policy based primarily on military intervention through counter-insurgency doctrines that focused on destroying the enemy through force and coercion. Though class consciousness grew throughout the 1950s, the internal violence of the time was not communist in nature since it had no true communist ideology holding the separate guerrillas together at the time. They were substantially more so bandits and non-ideologically aligned guerrilla self-defense forces than communists. However, because of the obvious conflict and disparity between the haves and have-nots, the potential for these armed groups to turn to communist ideology was substantial.

Many of the country's problems at the time were rooted in what could be considered a revolutionary situation among the have-nots. The history of military power, economic production and distribution, and political monopoly of the traditional élites in Colombia proved to serve mostly the country's oligarchy. Considering this situation, the traditional parties, though had been feuding violently against one another during La Violencia, decided to unite forces against the one threat that could potentially remove them from their traditional pedestal. The National Front was partly negotiated by both party members to contain the communist threat; thereby implementing a U.S.-backed military solution to deal with the problem. The National Front neglected to consider the concerns of a large portion of the Colombian population for the sake of maximizing wealth, dominance, and the interests of multi-national corporations, the U.S., and the Colombian oligarchy. As a result, such acts increased the potential for the adoption of a communist ideology by the resentful, violently opporessed, and marginalized have-nots.

By the 1960s, the stage was set for the spread of communist insurgency. With a newly acquired class consciousness by the peasantry, the mass inequality between the haves and the have-nots, the National Front's explicit exclusion of different political perspectives from the traditional Liberal/Conservative system, the government's lacking desire to take on the question of agrarian reform with sincerity, Colombia's alignment with the U.S.'s communist containment strategy, and the manner in which the state used force to subdue its opposition, the environment was ripe for an armed counter-movement. In the early stages of the insurgency, four different guerrilla groups are worthy of mention—National Liberation Army (ELN); Revolutionary Armed Forces of Colombia (FARC); People's Liberation Army (EPL); and 19th of April Movement (M-19).

The escalating events of La Violencia and the National Front combined with increasing Western economic, political, and military influence created a fertile soil for armed insurgency as a form of conflict resolution. By restricting political participation to the views of the traditional oligarchy, the concerns and grievances of the poor, who amounted to most of the Colombian population, could not be entertained with much hope for peaceful change. The institutions put in place to keep such a system intact bred resentment and a strong desire for justice, reform, and revolution. The use of force and the lack of state legitimacy produced a situation of fear, mistrust, and dissatisfaction.

The National Front's fear of potentially becoming another Cuba led the government to collaborate with the U.S. to train Colombia's security forces in counter-insurgency operations. Since both the traditional Colombian oligarchs and the U.S. wanted to stop the spread of communism, they actively reacted against real and potential leftist rebels. In Colombia, Plan LASO—a Latin American security operation in the 1960s—was created to destroy the military and social infrastructure of the guerrillas and communists. There was a strong fear that the "independent republics" of the leftist insurgents—created during the oppressive times of La Violencia and the National Front—would generate a greater security threat to the interests of the traditional system.

In May of 1964, during the final phase of Plan LASO, the U.S. (indirectly) and Colombian forces (directly) conducted "Operation Marquetalia," which was meant to militarily overrun the Marquetalia Republic. The U.S. and Colombia understood that Jacobo Arenas, one of the main leaders of the

60

Marquetalia Republic and charismatic Marxist ideologue, wanted to turn the rebel settlement into a socialist commune in the style of the Paris Commune of 1871 and of the Chinese Revolution of 1949. With the help of Manuel Marulanda Vélez, a peasant activist in his mid-thirties whose consciousness was awakened during La Violencia, these communes were to be organized in a way that they could be self-sufficient economically and well-defended militarily. Due to the recent success of the Cuban Revolution in 1959, Colombia did not want to take any chances (nor did the U.S.). It is estimated that nearly 16,000 Colombian security officers participated in "Operation Marquetalia," which used heavy artillery, infantry, police, and bomber aircraft to drop napalm bombs.[56] The aftermath of this operation is recognized as the birth of the FARC.

The spread of communist insurgency

Efforts to contain the spread of communist ideals created more of a justification for communism than ever before. As claimed during the First Southern Guerrilla Conference of 20 July 1964, the guerrillas considered themselves "victims of the policy of fire and sword proclaimed and carried out by the oligarchic usurpers of power," which ultimately called for "armed revolutionary struggle to win power."[57] The counter-insurgency attacks were recognized by the leftists rebels, peasants, and those affected and displaced by government security forces and death squads to be using coercion and force against Colombian citizens to secure Colombian capitalist and foreign interests at the expense of Colombia's poor and marginalized populations. In short, the have-nots saw the counter-insurgency measures as neglecting the economic and political concerns and necessities of the Colombian people for the sake of global imperialism. Because of the seemingly impossible task of changing policy and the exploitative, coercively oppressive system via peaceful, legal, and political avenues, some of country's oppressed poor and vulnerable populations decided the only remaining option was armed struggle.

The FARC, led by Marulanda and Arenas, however, were not the only guerrilla group to evolve out of the new situation on the ground. Inspired by the success of the Cuban Revolution of the 1950s, the ELN also emerged as one of the first unified Colombian insurgency organizations during the Cold War. The group was founded by young members of the Colombia Communist Party (PCC) in 1964. The founding members were trained in Castro's Cuba. Like other guerrilla organizations to come, in the early days its main sources of income came from extortion, kidnapping, robberies, and voluntary contributions from those members of civil society partial to what the group tried to accomplish. The ELN differentiated itself from Fidel Castro's communism and the FARC in that it was a hybrid between Marxism and Liberation Theology. This new Latin American Catholic political movement took on the teachings of Jesus Christ and focused on changing the economic and political liberal system of the time that was said to be a significant cause of most of the injustices occurring in the region. The group saw a direct correlation between the capitalist system, Western imperialism, and the suffering of the poor. Succeeding Catholic priests aligned with the radical ideas of Liberation Theology and revolutionary praxis led the group. These priests were publicly critical of Colombia's political and economic system and claimed that it was the reason for the grossly unequal distribution of wealth and power throughout the country. Operating mostly in the country's Northeast, its membership grew to a few hundred by the end of the decade. By the 1970s, the ELN had survived heavy blows in encounters with the Colombian military. They continued their practice of armed attacks against the country's infrastructure, petroleum companies (both domestic and foreign), and ransom kidnappings. As the illicit drug trade started to shift more heavily to Colombia, so too did the ELN's involvement (as well as the involvement of the other insurgent groups) in taxing narco-trafficking. (I will later explain the role of narco-trafficking.)

Though both the FARC and ELN continued to grow, the FARC mainly in the South and the ELN in the Northeast, neither group was able to create an area secured from the intrusion of the Colombian Armed Forces. Nevertheless, other insurgent organizations did follow suit, such as the EPL and M-19. By 1967, a splinter group from the Marxist-Leninist Communist Party of Colombia (PCC-ML) founded the EPL. They differed from their predecessors due to their affiliation with the Chinese. This insurgency was mostly Maoist inspired and was even able to receive support from China. Nevertheless, the movement remained small around the Medellín outskirts, attaining between 200 and 300 members. The M-19, on the other hand, though got a late start, was able to grow to nearly 2,000 guerrillas by the mid-1980s. The M-19 was founded in 1970 and operated mainly in Colombia's Southern and Center regions. The spark for its existence was the alleged fraudulent presidential elections of 1970 that allowed the National Front to continue dominating politics. Interestingly, the politician who was allegedly denied victory was former dictator Rojas Pinilla, then running for the National Popular Alliance (ANAPO). Rojas ran as an opposition candidate with a populist stance. It was the Electoral Court's ruling against Rojas, after the election results were officially challenged, that spawned the M-19—named after the day of the election (19th of April). Aside from populism, the movement was founded on a nationalism guided by revolutionary socialism.

National Front policies in the 1970s helped these communist insurgent organizations gain momentum and popular support. The government focused on getting rid of investment barriers throughout the countryside. In the process, the ownership of land became even more concentrated in the hands of the traditional oligarchs at the expense of peasants and their small-scale projects. This kind of development model forced peasants to leave the countryside to try to find work in major cities. Ill-equipped for city life and city jobs combined with limited jobs caused urban unemployment to rise. This new form of urbanization through industrialization created the foundation for the National Civic Strike of 1977, which was partly responsible for the following year's Draconian Security Statute that ended up greatly limiting the rights of workers to organize and protest.

The communist insurgency began to represent to the proletariat what Gaitán represented to the poor before La Violencia. To those who fought for workers' rights, agrarian reform, and were critical of politicians who favored the U.S. and Colombian oligarchy interests over those of the common Colombian, Gaitán embodied the hope of millions for democratic change. With Gaitán, the people believed there was a possibility their cries would be heard and that the traditional Liberal and Conservative parties would be forced to listen to the people's demands and concerns once and for all. By the early 1980s, the guerrillas had become a new hope for change.

The 1980s crisis

During this period, the FARC grew from around 500 members in 1970 to nearly 3,000 guerrillas in 1982. As a direct result of what occurred during the previous decades, the FARC, other guerrilla organizations, and the political Left began to gather increasing public support. In 1982, during their Seventh Guerrilla Conference, the FARC added the initials "EP" to its name—Ejército del Pueblo/People's Army—to be considered a legitimate rebel army and not simply a guerrilla group. Also, it set down a strategic plan to take over the government by the 1990s through a Marxist and Communist strategy understood as "the combination of all forms of struggle." For the first time in its history it was not only a self-defense organization but finally had the numbers and fire power to offensively pose a threat to government control. The strategy was to combine both military and political struggles. With this plan, and a new

64

opportunity in the mid-1980s from the Betancur administration for political inclusion, the FARC identified itself as "an alternative distinct from the traditional parties and in pursuit of paths other than the war."[58]

Understanding the growing popularity of the FARC, on October of 1984, then President Belisario Betancur (1982-1986) initiated a cease-fire with the FARC.[59] By May of 1985, the government had allowed the FARC to form a legitimate political party, the Unión Patriótica (UP),[60] and by August of 1986 they were recognized as a political movement by the National Electoral Council. The long-standing legacy of the National Front was diminishing. This legitimacy did not last for long, however. Pablo Escobar's MAS (Muerte a Secuestradores/Death to Kidnappers), the Castaño brothers' right-wing paramilitaries, other death squads, and even the government's armed forces—seeing themselves attacked also politically by the UP, which was winning more and more seats in municipal and national elections—decided to take violent action to annihilate the new political party. The mass assassinations made it so the UP no longer has status as a political party and has not since 2002. This can be directly attributed to political genocide, as over 2,000 (low estimate; 5,000 according to the FARC) members and sympathizers—legislators, mayors, and even presidential candidates—were murdered or disappeared since 1984.[61]

The UP stood on a communist and Marxist foundation, as could be expected since most members were of the Colombian Communist Party (PCC) and the FARC. As an alternative to the two main ruling parties in Colombia, the UP focused on bettering the lives of the poor. The political genocide sent the message to the FARC that its goals could not materialize by political means.[62] The FARC understood that if Colombia was to sincerely tackle issues of economic and political exclusion and social dislocation, violence was the only logical remaining route. The sincerity of the government's cease fire and opening for peaceful negotiations was questioned by the FARC, UP members, and sympathizers, and when time came to negotiate during the César Gaviria administration (1990-1994), the FARC opted out. Between 1990 and 1994, four guerrilla organizations (including the M-19 and EPL) signed peace agreements for political reconciliation—many were included into the political system under new political parties, which new agreements and pardons allowed. Nevertheless, the FARC—and ELN—grew more and more certain that in Colombia a peaceful transformation of politics and the economic system could only come through the barrel of the gun.

The 1980s, however, did not only mark the rise of communist guerrillas as a real threat to the state, but introduced other problematic illegally armed forces. Since the state lacked hegemony and a monopoly of force, many of the large landowners and corporations were left without protection. To fill the power vacuum, paramilitary groups, created and funded by right-wing large landowners, began to sprout throughout the country. Simultaneously, the illicit drug trade began to increase in Colombia, making its cartels (Medellín Cartel and Cali Cartel, for example) some of the most feared and powerful in the world. Ideologically speaking, the interests of the paramilitaries were very much aligned with those of the traditional two-party system. Since the state military was weak and not modernized, it often collaborated with the paramilitary organizations to combat the guerrillas. The drug cartels, too, had interests that led to violent clashes with all other armed groups. Pablo Escobar and his Medellín Cartel's total war against the government illustrates how vulnerable and desperate the state was becoming by the 1990s.

All illegally armed groups and a significant percentage of state institutions—because of corruption and desperation—were impacted by narco-trafficking. Money was laundered, used to finance clientelism and other forms of corruption, and was funneled throughout guerrilla and paramilitary ranks. The 1980s left the country in a crisis of authority and hegemony where all major actors and institutions of the time could not be said to have legitimacy, and conflict resolution was led by coercive measures. The 1990s began with an ineffective state

- unable to establish sovereignty,
- that lacked a monopoly of force,
- unable to effectively develop and distribute public goods and property rights,
- unable to resist corruption, and
- an armed opposition that was going nowhere.

It was within this landscape—a fragmented sovereignty with infrastructural weakness and reactionary (paramilitary; drug cartels) and revolutionary (guerrilla) armed movements—that the Colombian state decided to officially usher in laissez faire economic liberalism as part of its new 1990s development policy.

** ** ** ** ** ** ** ** ** ** ** **

From the early 1800s through the end of the Cold War, Colombia's ineffectiveness as a nation-state was closely linked to its historical lack of hegemony and institutionalized violence. The combination of a historically fragmented sovereignty, the lack of a professional national army, limited police presence, lack of power-sharing mechanisms that included minority groups, the state's blatant disregard for taking the interests of most Colombians seriously when making policy, and the view of violence being the most flagrant manifestation of power had horrific results. The early moments that led up to revolution against colonial Spain and the first eight decades of Colombia's liberated history is demarcated by dozens of rebellions, revolts, and civil wars. Unlike the 19th century when the two traditional parties mostly feared each other, the 20th century brought forth new threats, both foreign and domestic, to the two political parties, who tried desperately and aggressively to hold on to the traditional system of oligarchic, patriarchal, and white supremacy power.

Northern imperialism, the communist threat, the Western push for economic liberalism, and the global illicit drug trade added new elements to the already complex and bloody history of a country that after nearly two centuries still tried to learn how to, in the words of El Libertador Bolívar, extricate the nascent republic from chaos.

Where Have All Colombia's Disappeared Gone?

28 March 2011, *Colombia Reports*

The current Colombian administration denies the kidnapping, torture, and murder of thousands of citizens. In an interview this past Wednesday, 23 March, Defense Minister Rodrigo Rivera spoke with certainty about what he called a definitive reduction of violence and delinquency. This so-called "certainty" is worrisome, as there is nothing certain about the topic since there are so many disappeared persons in Colombia.

If an individual is disappeared, the whereabouts and what may have occurred to the person is most likely unknown (or, at least, not included as a numerical statistic in a row or column not labeled *disappeared*). Nevertheless, if we are to look at our own history or the history of other countries hit with high levels of forced disappearances—like Chile and Argentina in the 20th century—then we can at least infer a significant number of such disappeared individuals were most likely subjected to crimes against humanity and human rights violations that, by any statistical measure, would be recognized as an increase in violence, not a reduction.

When journalists asked Mr. Rivera point blank about the many critiques he has received regarding security in Colombia, he responded with the following statement:

> The statistics clearly show an improvement, a reduction in crime. But we are in an election year, we are in a time when citizens rightly claim the events that happen in certain places. I believe that a society that protests against crime is a society that has the basic element to be successful on offense. I would worry if people were indifferent. Before, there was no concept of security. Ten years ago, that didn't exist.

But the person being indifferent is Mr. Rivera. There are (at least) three things that are alarming with his statement. First, instead of directly addressing the critiques brought against him, Rivera passed the blame to it being an election year and that we should be happy people are even talking about security. This move directly avoids the legitimate concern regarding the statement that crime has "clearly" been reduced.

If anything, Mr. Rivera should unpack and elaborate on the claim. What kind of crime? How is he defining crime? Have all manifestations of crime been reduced? Have other forms of crime seen an increase? What periods is Mr. Rivera comparing to claim with such certainty that the statistics clearly illustrate a decrease in crime? And so on.

Second, it is irresponsible to always compare current Colombia to a time in the country's history when becoming a failed state seemed inevitable and unavoidable. Why not compare today's Colombia to the Colombia of 2007, 2008, 2009, or 2010, instead of the situation in the late 1990s and early 21st century when the country was on the verge of collapsing because of an internal armed conflict? The Colombia of the past four years is a better comparison when we look at today's Colombia, even for the sole reason that during those years talk of "security" existed—as Mr. Rivera already claimed—and that this range of years is a better sample for comparison to 2011 when we look at reasonably immediate fluctuations in crime.

And, third, if we do compare security and crime to these more recent years, what will we find? Will we find statistics that clearly show an improvement in a reduction of crime and delinquency? No, we do not find clarity, especially if we zone in on recent statistics of those identified as disappeared.

Though we cannot be sure what happened to disappeared individuals (e.g., torture, murder, kidnapping, runaways), an April 2009 preliminary report by the Colombian Justice and Peace Unit of the Prosecutor General declared that almost 50,000 Colombians have been identified as disappeared/missing. This contradicts the previous government figure of only 10,584 missing persons. Other reports by groups such as Latin American Working Group (LAWG) claimed the figure is much higher than 50,000. The 2009 Prosecutor General's 2009 finding is almost double the figure of disappeared persons in Argentina during its Dirty War. If the experiences from Argentina's *desaparecidos* are any indication of what may have occurred to Colombia's missing persons, we can be sure human rights violations on every level have occurred.

The term *desaparecido*, as Marguerite Feitlowitz suggested in her book *A Lexicon of Terror: Argentina and the Legacies of Torture*, is "a way of denying the kidnap, torture, and murder of thousands of citizens." As Primo Levi, in *The Drowned and the Saved*, pointed out after his experience at the hands of the Nazis, the three purposes of concentrationary systems are "slave work [...] elimination of political adversaries and the extermination of the so-called inferior races." Much of what

Feitlowitz and Levi wrote rings true to what is going on in Colombia: forced disappearances are occurring for similar reasons as Levi suggested (human cleansing campaigns, elimination of those who threaten the attainment of self or group interests, etc.). Further, in line with Feitlowitz's view about the term "disappeared" used by governments, the Santos administration uses the term (or does not even use it, for that matter) to deny the "kidnap, torture, and murder of thousands of citizens."

Defense Minister Rivera cannot be as certain as he is that violence, delinquency, and crime have clearly improved. I repeat, he cannot claim this with certainty when in 2007 there were 4,323 disappeared, when in 2008 there were 15,696, and while in 2009 there was yet another increase to 18,236 disappeared. Assuming these statistics paint at least a partial truth, just in those three years—an increasing trend, mind you—there were 38,255 disappearances. If they are disappeared, and he recognizes there are disappeared persons in Colombia, then Mr. Rivera CANNOT be certain that such an improvement in the security of the country is happening.

But even the statistics from 2007 to 2009 do not yield clarity and certainty. The numeric value of 38,255 does not amount to a rise in disappearances, but the amount of reported complaints. After the paramilitaries demobilized, more people felt they could file a report on old cases. These old cases distort the numbers. However, though we cannot be certain, when *Colombia Reports* staff, for example, goes out to talk to people in the popular *comunas* of Medellín and other neighborhoods of the city, what the people report to us suggests at least two things: (1) People are still being disappeared and (2) some are still afraid to report complaints of disappearances.

One woman with whom I spoke, whose husband was disappeared just weeks before in September, told me that on her block alone three people had disappeared within three weeks. Further, I spoke to another woman only a month ago—who was displaced in Medellín because of death threats—who alleged there was a mass grave in her *comuna* of about 15 persons of which the government is not aware. The reason for the government's lack of knowledge? Though many of the friends and family members of the missing persons know exactly where their loved ones are buried and whose hands dug the graves, they do not speak up because they fear they too may become a disappeared—displaced, kidnapped, tortured, killed, and buried in a common mass grave.

What does this mean? It means Mr. Rivera's claim of certainty is clearly ill-founded, as it is based on the following: (a) limited, distorted, and/or false evidence; (b) illogical reasoning; and/or (c) a desire to manipulate and mislead. You be the judge.

My tone is angry because a government that withholds information to manipulate its citizenry is a government that lies to its people, which is exactly what is going on here. For what reason is the government trying to manipulate us? I can only speculate, as Mr. Rivera already has (up-coming elections?). But it is obvious the lack of transparency and the picking and choosing of statistics to disseminate to the public is selective and calculated. We need to ask the right questions to unpack the layers a little more, and to potentially catch a glimpse of a glimmer of truth.

I am looking at the statistics, Mr. Rivera, and the only way your statement may potentially make any sense is by neglecting to consider any disappeared persons in your assessment of reduction of crime in Colombia. It is obvious that if one does not know what happened to a disappeared person, that individual cannot be explicitly inserted into a statistic of, for example, homicide or kidnapping. However, to not even publicly consider the possibility that such large number of disappeared persons could very well be part of that statistic (as Colombian history clearly suggests this is a great possibility), then we are being mistreated with data forwarded to misinform and mislead the public.

This being an election year, a misinformed citizenry will most likely vote for individuals and policies that harm them, the city, and the state if such manipulation continues because things are not as peach-y-keen as you, Mr. Rivera, would like us to believe. Only by recognizing an ailment can we begin treatment. Pretending there isn't a problem will not make the problem disappear.

For this reason, I claim that the administration the Defense Minister represents is denying the kidnapping, torture, and murder of thousands of citizens, in turn lying to us, trying to manipulate and sell us a portrait of "security" that does not exist and that every day looks more and more like a painting from the French Impressionist painters—where there is slight emphasis on the accurate depiction of light (truth/reality) in its changing qualities—than a piece of realism art whose effort is to depict objective reality, without embellishment or interpretation.

Colombia's 'Obligatory' Military Service: The Arbitrary Role of Class Disparity

25 July 2011, *Colombia Reports*

When Álvaro Uribe Vélez first ran for president of Colombia, journalists, politicians, and civil society did not press a question I thought important. When asked why he and his sons had never performed military service, his campaign declined to comment. The shadow of this question remains indelible in my mind. This is the case not just because Uribe and his sons may have bribed their way into avoiding the country's obligatory military conscription service for males. It is also because there is a systemic problem regarding the process of stocking our armed forces and the explicit unfairness of legislation weighed against the poor. It is legislation that, in many ways, holds the poor hostage and extracts forced labor from the lower classes of Colombian society. More politicians, governments, and journalists need to nurture and raise this issue more often and more forcefully, but it does not surprise me the matter remains largely uncultivated.

Like Uribe's avoidance of the question during his campaign, the reason why this issue has not become mainstream may be because most eligible politicians for obligatory military conscription—and potentially also their sons—have also dodged the service in an illegal manner or do not want the current laws favoring the wealthy to change. If we truly want to justly govern ourselves, we must start with (1) revising legislation that is so explicitly against most of the population, with (2) judicially cracking down on those who bribe their way out of the armed conflict's frontier, and with (3) the international community recognizing its role and changing its ways in this unfair and unjust practice.

Who makes up Colombia's armed forces? Overwhelmingly the poor. I will not tackle the issue of whether Colombia should have obligatory military conscription or a volunteer army. However, considering the former is our current situation—obligatory military conscription—should not our armed forces represent the entire spectrum of our economic classes and the stratification of our civil society? Unfortunately, the reflection is like a fun house mirror that distorts reality and makes our upper classes almost invisible in the country's military. If they are present, they are mostly in cushy positions. As Francisco Santos stated during the 2002 presidential elections, "Right now, the poorest of the poor do the fighting, and the rich people drive the generals' cars, if anything."

When we speak of our country's (in)security, we hurdle over the question of how we construct our armed forces in the first place, and we run head-on into a discourse of how we should use that army and the funding it is allotted. However, if we want to transform Colombia's political and armed conflict, we should underscore this deserving issue and give it priority potentially even before, or at least during, negotiations and

76

discussions on military budgets, increasing our armed forces, and the overall development of tactics and strategies that deal with the country's security threats and issues.

Furthermore, the assumption that our army is formed in a just and fair manner needs to stop before foreign (and domestic) military assistance is provided. Colombia's conflict is not solely a domestic issue. Its tentacles cross not only the country's borders via a spill-over effect, its tentacles reach not only where Colombia's illicit drugs are consumed, but also the policies of other countries on Colombia—like the current U.S. war on narco-terrorism.

In 2002, the relationship between Washington, D.C., and Bogotá grew stronger after Uribe took office. Both seats of power had common interest in militarizing Colombia. The Colombian armed forces went through a rapid process of modernization, resulting in an increase of armed forces members. Though the U.S. has been recognized by some as losing influence on its traditional backyard with the move of many South American countries to the left of center, its influence on Colombia for the better part of the 21st century remained quite powerful. Some Colombian politicians have even publicly recognized that if the U.S. did not have so much influence, a policy such as Plan Colombia would not have materialized the way it did. Instead, it would have looked more like Andres Pastrana originally conceived—a Marshall Plan for Colombia where developed countries could help offer "peasants different alternatives to the illicit crops" through social investments. Sergio Fajardo, for example, while he campaigned for the presidency in 2009 claimed that though it would be better for Colombia if certain illicit drugs were legalized, it would be political suicide to run on such a platform.

Nevertheless, there seems to be a seemingly unexpected rhetorical shift in policy with President Juan Manuel Santos.

His administration has pushed the U.S., the region, and the world to have a new dialogue on the U.S. decades-long strategy of targeting the issue where these illicit drugs are grown. Though he has flat out rejected the idea of legalization, even President Barak Obama's Drug Czar, Gil Kerlikowske, supported focusing more energy on U.S demand for illicit drugs. However, there is still much to be done. Though there have been slight shifts, in terms of Colombia's militarization and how we stock our armed forces, not much has changed. Certain kinds of crimes have been on the rise during recent years, and the FARC, ELN, and neo-paramilitaries continue to threaten national security.

In March, Defense Minister Rodrigo Rivera claimed that "The statistics clearly show an improvement, a reduction of crime." In early April, the previous secretary of government stated that the BACRIM (criminal bands) did not exist within Bogotá. More recently, on 30 June, on their hearing on the state of democracy in the Americas, even the U.S. Senate Committee in Foreign Relations Subcommittee on Western Hemisphere, Peace Corps, and Global Narcotics Affairs sided with Rivera. In the previous few weeks, however, other major Colombian government officials have come out declaring the opposite.

Along with the increase in attempted and/or actual bombings in cities around the country, the new secretary of government, Mariella Barragan Beltran, admitted the presence of BACRIM in the capital. The Medellín ombudsman stated that his city's displacement could double in 2011. President Juan Manuel Santos himself even publicly recognized the deterioration of the security situation in Colombia.

Either the security situation has deteriorated dramatically since Rivera's declaration back on 23 March, or he lied to us (probably to not scare away investors, tourists, and because of October elections), as I argued in one of my previous columns. Either way, this arena of insecurity will most likely call for an increase in the number of armed forces members. A request for a heavier fist yields a greater burden the poor must carry. As *Washington Post* foreign service correspondent Scott Wilson in 2002 correctly identified, the "rich avoid the draft as the poor are pulled into the trenches."

While the poor fight in the incessant internal conflict, the wealthy continue to benefit from the system as the army is used to protect many of the élite's interests. Individuals with a high school diploma must only serve one year of service, while those without one are forced to serve 18 to 24 months. The majority of those who serve 18 to 24 months are the poor masses, living largely in the poor communities of the country. Furthermore, while in some cases it is legal for those who have the monetary means to buy a military service record, many of the poor cannot afford the legal purchase of the military card or even a bribe. This record is meant to eliminate the requirement to serve in the military. Individuals who do not have a military service record cannot graduate from university, own property, obtain a passport, enter into a legal work contract, and are considered deserters. About half of the individuals who are obliged to perform military service refuse, and more than 1,800 physically desert the army annually. Depending on the situation, a deserter may be penalized with imprisonment for a time span ranging from three months to four years, which is usually followed by starting or resuming military service.

Not until recently was substitute service available for conscientious objectors. For years, it was argued that the institutionalized practice of forced recruitment went against Article 18 of the 1991 Colombian Constitution, which states the following: "The freedom of conscience is guaranteed. Nobody will be bothered by reason of his convictions nor beliefs neither compelled to reveal them nor obliged to act against his conscience." However, Article 18 conflicts with Article 216, whereby it is states that

> All Colombian citizens are obliged to take up arms when
> there is a public need for this to defend national
> independence and the public institutions. The law will
> determine the conditions which at all times qualifies an
> individual for exemption from military service and the
> benefits for service in them.

The former Article now trumps the latter. In September 2010,
the Colombian Constitutional Court ruled that conscientious
objectors have the right to be exempt from the duty of serving
in Colombia's obligatory military service if the objections of
these individuals are judged to be "deep, fixed, and sincere."
Though this is a step in the right direction for transforming the
political conflict toward just governance, there are other
government practices of military recruitment, like arbitrary
detention and the others already mentioned above, that
continue to unjustly target the poor.

It is well understood that illegal recruitment is commonplace.
These recruitment practices—raids referred to as *batidas*—are
forced and have been constituted by the UN as forms of
arbitrary detention. A significant number of the poor are
forcibly detained on the streets, at bus stops, and market
places, and then taken to recruitment centers and barracks
where they are forced to perform military service. Since these
recruits are considered deserters, they are then taken to
different locations around the country to conflict areas, even
though it is clear under Law No. 48 that they are supposed to
perform their "duty" in their local areas. In these cases, the
exploitation of Colombia's poor is evident while many of the
privileged fortunate individuals born into wealth continue to
have the opportunity to opt out or not be targeted for
detention.

Because of such practices, policies, legislation, and an almost
lethargic judiciary when it comes to investigating potential
cases of illegal attainments of military service records, the poor
continue to carry the burden of Colombia's conflict.

Colombia's history is marked with many of its people treated merely as a mean to an end. Laura Yusem and Herbert Braun, respectively, were right in recognizing that "In Latin America, we learn early that our lives are worth little" and that "[i]n the struggle for land, human life in Colombia has been devalued." Human rights activist Manuel Rozental was correct to paint Colombia's history with the following pattern: people are massacred or enslaved, displaced, the land is freed, and the élite, foreign powers, and multi-national corporations come in to exploit the land and the labor force.

The recruitment practices and blind eyes of our branches of government, media outlets, and the international community are nothing more than part of this historical pattern. In short, many Colombian lives are treated with little importance—as if they are mere instruments, commodities, or replaceable and expendable objects—and used to maximize the power and the wealth of a select few. This needs to change for a more just and fair society to flourish in Colombia. We cannot allow this issue to die after a politician declines to comment when asked why he—or his or her son(s)—never partook in Colombia's so-called obligatory military service.

Uribe's Empty Apology

31 August 2010, *Colombia Reports*

Those of you glued to the television or the internet two weeks ago to see if Miss Colombia would be crowned Miss Universe for the second time in the country's history were probably greatly disappointed. Sadly, she did not even make it to the top ten, but Colombians are proud, nonetheless. Who caught my eye, however, was not the lovely Natalia Navarro, but Miss Philippines. Actually, it wasn't Miss Philippines herself so much as the politics behind why she went from being the shoo-in for the crown to finishing fourth.

Miss Philippines made a mistake—quite possibly the only mistake this woman has ever made. During the question and answer portion of the pageant—the last hurdle to jump before the judges would have placed the tiara on her head—judge William Baldwin asked a question that put everything up to this point into perspective, which suggested that political laws may also rule the realm of aesthetics. Baldwin asked, "What is one big mistake you have made in your life, and what did you do to make it right?" She responded with almost blind confidence, "You know what, sir, in my 22 years of existence, I can say there is nothing major, major, I mean problem, that I have done in my life."

One thing was clear: the judges were not happy with her answer. It was not that there was a right answer, but hers was just not the answer they sought. I wasn't a judge, so I can't be certain, but I am willing to guess her response did not sit well with the judges—and, I imagine, with many viewers, as well— because she probably lied. If she didn't lie, then she was most likely delusional about her life since it is difficult to believe a human being, regardless of how beautiful, can go through "22 years of existence" without ever making a big mistake. She would have been better off answering the question honestly, which does not mean she would have had to bare her soul to, well, the universe.

Baldwin's question was built around the sophisticated assumption that humans are not perfect. I will give her the benefit of the doubt and suggest that maybe, just maybe, she believed she had made little mistakes along the way, but nothing major. The excuse I offer her with this proposition, however, does not change the fact she made a mistake in the judges' eyes with her answer. In short, she lost the hearts and minds of her royal subjects. And that, my friends, cannot be regained with a sparkling smile.

It is not just beauty queens who have this to fear, and a crown and public to lose. Miss Philippines is not alone in failing to be truthful about her imperfections. Few of us want to admit to mistakes, even though we all know we have made them. The beauty pageant is not too dissimilar from the political stage in this regard. You'd be hard-pressed to find many Colombian politicians willing to tell you the errors of their ways with any sincerity, if at all. That is, unless it served some instrumental purpose to a selfish end. In a country where blame and responsibility are passed around more often than the pepper shaker during a family reunion dinner, admitting one's flaws can go a long way. Doing so is an opportunity for reconciliation.

For instance, George W. Bush, during his final moments as president, had the opportunity to quell many fires of resentment, if only he had honestly answered the same question Miss Philippines was asked. Instead, his response was, "Hmmm, I wish you would have given me this as a written question ahead of time." Bush blew his chance. Not only did he imply he could not think of anything at that moment, but that if he had more time to think about it he may had come up with a reply more suitable for public consumption, more politically correct. Regardless of his intentions or the truth, his answer was interpreted by the world to mean he made no mistakes during his two terms in office as president of the United States. On top of the political and economic blunders and botched attempts of the U.S. military as it tried to, allegedly, safeguard the world from terrorism and spread the U.S. brand of democracy and freedom, this seemingly meaningless response had more weight than he, or anybody, may have imagined. It was not a good way to leave office.

Former Colombian President Álvaro Uribe Vélez had the same opportunity as Miss Philippines and Mr. Bush. In fact, he did not even need a judge or a reporter to ask him about his mistakes but addressed the issue when he went on public television during his final days to say goodbye to the nation and to reminisce about his eight years in office. For this, I congratulate Señor Uribe. Nevertheless, Uribe, too, blew his opportunity for reconciliation, and alienated listeners, like myself, even more.

Uribe gave the nation an apology, asked Colombians to forgive him for, as he put it, "Those errors that were committed, and also for those things that could not be done." And that was all. Newspaper headlines were littered with "Uribe's apology," and so forth. However, asking for forgiveness and apologizing for errors seem almost meaningless without any context or further information.

I am surprised that to this date, a good month since Uribe "apologized," there has not been much advanced for further clarification from pundits, reporters, and the public at large. As it stands, the apology remains anemic—"Gravy without the meat," as philosopher Nick Smith would say. It has sunk to the bottom of Laguna de Guatavita to be lost among the priceless artifacts of El Dorado. With this essay—or letter to Señor Uribe, if you will—I hope to begin, metaphorically speaking, to drain the cloudy water of the lake that keeps the golden meaning of Uribe's apology hidden from the public.

It is difficult to argue against the claim that Colombia became highly polarized during the reign of Señor Uribe. Everyone was either an Uribista or a terrorist sympathizer. Others, like Sergio Fajardo, tried to remove themselves from such rhetoric, being neither for or against the leader. The indigenous Minga had a similar neutrality stance. Or, as the residents of Algeciras recently demonstrated with their protest signs during an armed transport blockage by the FARC, when the residents claimed, "We want to work, this is not a demonstration against or in favor of anyone." Sadly, people were afraid to voice their political opinions for fear they may become another false positive, another victim kidnapped by the guerrilla, or a target of human cleansing by neo-paramilitary groups. Nonetheless, the polarization and hatred were the elephant in the room, and most wanted the elephant to stomp on the opposition.

Colombia has become—possibly more so than before, which is saying a lot—a country of people who harbor a lot of anger and resentment. To calm those kinds of fires will take more than military force alone, which is what Uribe's Democratic Security and Defense Policy mostly offered. There are certain areas of the armed conflict—or struggle, "lucha," as Señor Uribe likes to label it—that violence or the threat of violence cannot help. I believe Uribe understood this when he so generously offered his apology.

A lot of anger could be reduced by a simple recognition of wrongdoing by not only the government, but also the guerrillas and the paramilitaries. Colombia has many victims who look for more than just monetary reparation or penal punishment. Many want their injuries to be documented and blame to be distributed among the parties responsible for their suffering and losses.

This is an integral part of justice, of reconciliation, of conflict resolution. One does not have to wait to first establish security—understood by Uribe as a monopoly of violence— and gain capital investment as pre-requisites for taking social welfare concerns seriously, as Uribe's Democratic Security and Defense Policy assumed; the so-called "Virtuous Circle."

An apology is an essential means to begin the process of justice, reparation, and the corroboration of truth. Other heads of state were aware of the importance of apologies in soothing the aching hearts of the public. The Canadian prime minister did it in 2008 when he apologized for his country forcing First Nations children into residential schools; British Prime Minister David Cameron recently apologized for Bloody Sunday; and Japan's prime minister last month apologized for his country's colonial rule of Korea for 35 years. Though there are limitations to collective apologies, these acts had social meaning that opened the door for peace. The First Nations, for example, accepted Harper's apology, and family members of the victims of Bloody Sunday rejoiced knowing the names of their lost relatives were cleared of wrongdoing.

As philosopher Nick Smith—one of the world's leading expert on the matter—wrote, apologies have a social function. They present an opportunity to honor the meaning and values of a people. Apologies provide a tool for moral reconciliation because, as he claimed, they have both inherent and instrumental value. They act as "loose constellations of interrelated meanings," and by understanding what meanings are violated we can more effectively progress in resolving conflicts. Military force alone cannot repair such moral injuries. This was why Uribe's apology was so important, but, simultaneously, so anemic.

In my interview with Smith, his initial reaction to Uribe's apology was one of curiosity. Uribe's statement, Smith said, "leaves us guessing about the central meanings of the gesture. What were the errors? Who deserves blame for them? Will the errors be remedied? Will the future be different from the past?"

For Uribe's apology to sit well with me—one of the 50 million Colombians Uribe addressed, and others like me—at least some basic criteria need to be met. For starters, Señor Uribe would have to fully answer the questions Smith posed. And, as judge Baldwin asked Miss Philippines, what would he do to make things right?

Answers to all these inquiries could provide different forms of social meaning, which Uribe has failed to offer. Uribe apologized. Uribed asked for forgiveness. It is difficult to forgive an individual when he has not delivered a real apology. It is almost equally difficult to forgive someone who cannot explicitly explain the mistakes, the regret, the guilt, and the factors that led to the apology. Was Uribe really apologizing, or just expressing sympathy? Or, was he just upset that some of his mistakes were found out? If Uribe sincerely wants to be forgiven, he must unpack his apology. Let's start there.

Señor Uribe, for the good of the nation, I beg of you to answer the questions. Unlike Bush, you are getting them written, ahead of time. I hope you answer them sincerely, truthfully, and publicly in a robust manner. Señor Uribe, what exactly were "those errors that were committed"? And who, specifically, committed the errors? Señor Uribe, what exactly were "those things that could not be done"? As Smith puts it, "Rather than leaving [the apologizer and the recipients] reconciled because of the words spoken, I prefer to understand them as beginning a process of reconciliation." Señor Uribe, the opportunity is not lost.

As one citizen among many, I call upon you all to demand an answer from the former president. If you truly care about the unification and pacification of Colombia and wish to calm the fires of resentment, hatred, vengeance, and anger of this great country, you, the public, should demand this, and you, Señor Uribe, should respond.

Uribe's Pact of Silence Violates Academic Freedom

13 September 2010, *Colombia Reports*

Georgetown University has seen an outcry against Álvaro Uribe Vélez for his alleged institutional and human rights violations and against the university for appointing the former president as a guest lecturer, especially in such a secretive manner. With this piece I will not ride the coattails of this indignation. Instead, I bring to light something the mainstream media has not yet emphasized about Uribe and Georgetown.

Though not recognized by a world-renowned institution of higher education as a "distinguished scholar in the practice of global leadership," as Uribe is by Georgetown, I, too, am a university lecturer. Having dedicated my adult life to the academe, I am unsettled by Uribe's treatment of the spirit of our "sacred" institution.

At Georgetown, Uribe made students agree to a "pact of honor" to not disclose specific details about his lecture. Read the previous sentence again. Now consider it for a moment.

Such a request is worrisome. Not only does it place students in an awkward position, but also goes against the very spirit and purpose of university.

A university is an environment where ideas are forwarded, promoted, discussed, and debated. A university is a space for the search for truth, for the application of previous discoveries and wisdom, for challenging those curiosities. It is a place for the creation of new knowledge.

It is also a community where students and academics, together, are united by the principle that they are at university for learning and *sharing* these interpretations of truth and facts and histories *with* the outside world. A university is based on the notion of academic freedom.

Uribe did not advance such "sacred" and categorically imperative institutional mores and ethics. Instead, what he did introduce was an authoritarian restriction of these deep-rooted values and liberties.

The students had the choice to remain seated and accept Uribe's "pact of honor" and not disclose specific details about his lecture. The students also had the choice to not accept it and be escorted out.

However, I also believe these students still have the ability—even after attending—to breach the pact Uribe demanded, because it was an unjust request made by a representative of an institution of higher learning. Such a request attacks and assaults university principles.

If I would have been in the classroom when Uribe made the request, as I so much desired, I would have spoken up and challenged the proposed agreement. The possible responses to his "pact of honor" were not only "yes I accept" or "no I do not accept." Another answer would have been to oppose the very request as being, for a lack of a better term, unconstitutional.

Uribe's Georgetown "pact of honor" was an affront to the very intent of the institution that brought him there and that represents the students.

I would have countered Uribe with my own request, a "pact of honor" of a different sort: to remain in the classroom and abide by the spirit of university, or not lecture at all.

Though he was in a position of authority by being in front of the classroom as an invited lecturer, his authoritarianism crossed the line. He went above the rule of law of the institution that gave him the opportunity to speak.

Georgetown and Uribe should have never put the students in attendance in such a situation. Not only were the classroom and building already militarized with police and bodyguards because of Uribe's presence, but such a request must have made the atmosphere coercive, regardless of what the lecturer discussed and taught.

I am not challenging his ability to speak, but if he does speak, he must abide by the laws and rules of university, which he is not above. It makes me wonder what style of university Uribe wishes to establish in Colombia, as he recently suggested.

If any Georgetown students of Uribe read my words, I hope they have the courage to challenge this so-called "pact of honor" and respectfully remind Uribe he is not in Colombia anymore.

The Insecurity of Security Politics in the Andes: An Analysis of the U.S.-Colombian War on Narco-Terrorism and Its Impact on Colombia's Neighbors

On 9 October 2010, I presented this paper at the 2010 Congress of the Latin American Studies Association, in Toronto, Canada, for the panel titled Latin American Foreign Policies: South America and the U.S.

Introduction

Classic strategic literature on how a head of state should govern to secure the interests of both political society and civil society are as relevant as ever. Niccolò Machiavelli's advice in *The Prince* and *The Discourses* and Antonio Gramsci's writings on hegemony and transformation, for example, can help us understand why the Andean diplomatic crisis and security dilemma since the controversial Colombian raid on Ecuadorian territory may have escalated under former

Colombian President Álvaro Uribe Vélez but calmed with the leadership of current President Juan Manuel Santos. Though both Uribe and Santos put to practice Plan Colombia (PC) and Colombia's Democratic Security and Defense Policy (DSDP)—Santos himself was Uribe's Defense Minister during the March 2008 raid—and though both their agendas are aligned, as they are political realists and neo-liberals, Santos has applied different tactics than Uribe that are more effective from a diplomacy standpoint. In turn, Santos has better positioned himself for winning the hearts and minds of the people and neighbors than Uribe, or at least deescalating tensions, which may pave the way for realizing state goals more effectively.

Uribe's DSDP and allegiance to the United States brought the Andean region to a near armed confrontation and an alleged Cold War-styled arms race. This discussion concentrates on Colombia's diplomacy with Ecuador and Venezuela since March 1st, 2008, and this diplomacy's relationship to Colombia's U.S.-funded military fight against narco-terrorism and transnational delinquency. The main question I ask is the following: Why did Colombia stress regional security in the Andes under Uribe but not with Santos, though both implemented the U.S.-funded and U.S.-supported PC and DSDP? I argue that though PC and the DSDP under both Uribe and Santos share the same goals, Uribe and Santos emphasized different tactics for resolving conflicts domestically and regionally. Uribe's political realism was averse to critically thinking about the values and concerns of others. On the other hand, Santos's realism allows for taking the concerns of others seriously, even if the others are not as well-armed. In short, Uribe sacrificed the democratic element of the DSDP for the sake of security and defense. Santos, however, has moved closer toward respecting all three components of the policy, thereby demonstrating the will to peacefully reconcile and negotiate the conflict domestically and with neighboring states. What Santos has begun to bring to the table of diplomacy was missing during Uribe's reign, which was a detriment to Colombia's political society, civil society, and relationship with regional states.

I commence by summarizing PC—the main policy that has justified U.S. intervention in the Andes region—alongside the DSDP. PC and the DSDP will provide the context for unpacking the Andean diplomatic crisis and security dilemma. Thereafter, I provide an outline of a summary of relevant Machiavellian and Gramscian advice for Colombia's "Princes" to use as our interpretive lenses for evaluating Uribe's implementation of the DSDP against Santos's. The analysis leads us to conclude that the use of force, or threat of force, alone, at the expense of consent, cannot effectively secure state interests, as Machiavelli and Gramsci suggested. Winning over the will, hearts, and minds of the people and neighbors is also of primary importance in the endeavor—a variable we must not dismiss, neglect, or ignore.

Plan Colombia (PC) and Uribe's Democratic Security and Defense Policy (DSDP)

Fearing Colombia would become a failed state—especially after a Switzerland-sized territory was granted to the FARC (Revolutionary Armed Forces of Colombia) during negotiations with the Andrés Pastrana administration (1998-2002)—the U.S. introduced an interventionist policy in Colombia to subdue the insurgency through the U.S.-designed PC under the veil of combating the war on drugs. After 9/11 and the U.S. declaration of its war on terror, however, the veil was lifted, and PC officially became a counter-insurgency policy, not just a counter-narcotics operation. Twenty-first-century Colombia can be framed as being embroiled in a narco-terrorist war fully supported and partially financed by the U.S. The U.S. has interpreted PC as such an overwhelming success that the U.S. is currently using it as a blueprint for policy in the Afghanistan war and the violent drug war in Mexico. PC and Colombia's DSDP, advanced by Uribe, have become the exemplary strategies constituted to combat the internal armed conflict in the country in the twenty-first century.

Though PC was originally a fully Colombian proposal that recognized drugs as a social problem, in its final phase it was changed by the U.S. into a drug war on producers. In June of 1998, Colombian President Pastrana first conceived PC to be a Marshall Plan for Colombia where developed countries could help offer "peasants different alternatives to the illicit crops" through social investments. As originally presented, PC was "a set of alternative development projects which [would] channel the shared efforts of multilateral organizations and [foreign] governments towards Colombian society."[63] It was not meant to focus on trafficking, the modernization of the military, or the expansive aerial fumigation project that PC became.[64] Recognizing the country's violence was rooted in issues of profound economic disparity, violent political exclusion, and social dislocation, Pastrana's original concentration was to achieve peace by going straight to the root of Colombia's essential problems, which were social, political, and economic in nature. The violence and narco-trafficking for which Colombia is known are side-effects of a deeper malady. However, after meeting with then U.S. President Bill Clinton, PC became heavily influenced by U.S. concerns, thereby transforming it to center on military build-up and counter-narcotics by focusing on the source.

After Pastrana's negotiations with the FARC failed, Uribe's administrations took the Colombian throne with the platform that peace must now come by force and coercion. The U.S. fully supported the Uribe foundation, especially since Uribe's main success has become the modernization of Colombian Armed Forces and the weakening of the FARC. Uribe could not have militarized the country without funding, and it was to come "from wherever possible: assistance, external creditors, the pockets of Colombians."[65] All of the above materialized in the forms of a war tax,[66] an important increase of cost in military spending as percentage of GDP in comparison to previous decades,[67] and billions in foreign aid.[68] Most of the funding in the narco-terrorist war went to the country's military and police forces, with Colombia spending about $7 billion annually on the war.[69] When compared to international security and defense budget standards, the costs were really high, especially for the region. Most surprising was the 400 percent increased budget from Plan Colombia I to Plan Colombia II, especially since each program was set for a 6-year period.[70] As a result, Uribe was able to increase his combat-ready soldiers by more than 60 percent and modernized the Armed Forces like no previous administration.[71]

In fact, in the past decade, U.S. aid to Colombia via PC has been disproportionately concentrated on military and police modernization, averaging around 75%, while the rest has been distributed to institutional and, to a lesser extent, social programs.[72] Over $5 billion came from the U.S. alone during Uribe's tenure, and over $8 billion from Colombia itself since the implementation of PC a decade ago. Colombia is the largest recipient of U.S. military aid in the hemisphere, and up to the start of the Iraq invasion in March of 2003, Colombia was the third largest recipient in the world after Israel and Egypt. PC's U.S. funding helped militarize the country. In today's Colombia, the Uribe administrations' desire for total war against the opposition would not have been realized without U.S. intelligence, training, arms, technology, and military, political, and economic support.

Uribe's platform was prioritized as follows: (1) Establish a monopoly of violence throughout the entirety of Colombia to (2) secure capital investment. Only thereafter would (3) social welfare concerns be confronted. This was outlined by the Ministry of Defense annual report as Uribe's "Virtuous Circle": security investment → confidence and stability → private investment → economic growth → social investment → social welfare → security investment → and so on in the cycle.[73] Only by defeating illegally armed groups—with an obsessive focus on the FARC—could the welfare of the people be properly engaged.

The biggest concerns for Colombia, according to Uribe, were eradicating those he defined as narco-terrorists.[74] As stated during a 2004 interview, "Of course we need to eliminate social injustice in Colombia, but what is first? Peace. Without peace, there is no investment. Without investment, there are no fiscal resources for the government to invest in the welfare of the people."[75] During the World Economic Forum in April of 2010 held in Cartagena, Uribe echoed this sentiment when he said, "Those two elements, security and investment, help us finance social policies, so the country can overcome poverty, so the country can build equity."

To gain domestic dominance, Uribe militarized the country with his strategy for security and defense, which incorporated already existing PC. Uribe recognized the importance of security and self-interests and went about taking care of these basics human concerns primarily through a focus on the use and threat of violence to achieve desired goals. Fear is very prevalent in what motivates such realist security programs in that if the state is not capable of securing its interests, then a powerful actor (like the FARC) can take what the administration considers its own or what it desires to acquire. It was this basic fear of subjugation that drove Uribe and the U.S. to seek dominance. In turn, what took center stage was the challenge to secure the maneuvering capacity to produce effects over the Colombian territory and against others to safeguard interests, survival, and accomplish missions.

Aside from Uribe, no Colombian government official had ever been more determined to attain hegemony[76] than El Libertador, Simón Bolívar. He pronounced Spain the source of all Colombia's woes and suffering, injustices, and feelings of hatred and vengeance.[77] Bolívar's certainty on this issue was so intense that he promised himself and Colombia he would not stop fighting for Colombia's liberty, weapons at hand, until he "eradicate[d] every last Spaniard from the provinces [...] that have most recently experienced the excess of their tyranny, their injustice, their perfidy, and their atrocities."[78] He would not rest until the Spanish yoke was removed for good.[79] All those Spaniards on Colombian soil who would not join in the war against Spain were considered enemies, punished, and killed.[80] Bolívar saw no other option but to take up arms against Spain.[81] Narco-terrorists and those who opposed the DSDP were to Uribe what Spain was to Bolívar, and, thus, total war was inevitable. Even President Santos labelled Uribe Colombia's second Liberator.[82]

Uribe has also been praised abroad for his allegiance to the war on terror, democracy, and the alleged overwhelming success of his DSDP. He received the "Light unto the Nations" award by the American Jewish committee in May of 2007 for being "a staunch ally of the United States, a good friend of Israel and the Jewish people, and [...] a firm believer in human dignity and human development in Colombia and the Americas."[83] George W. Bush, in January 2009, awarded Uribe with the Medal of Freedom—the highest civilian honor the U.S. grants—for Uribe's "work to improve the lives of [Colombia's] citizens and for [his] efforts to promote democracy, human rights and peace abroad," and for being a "staunch all[y] of the United States, particularly combating terrorism."[84] On August 2010, the UN selected Uribe to vice chair a four-person team to lead the investigation regarding the Israeli flotilla raid incident of May 21st, 2010.[85] Georgetown University, in Washington, D.C., offered him a teaching position in 2010, recognizing him as a "distinguished scholar in the practice of global leadership." On October 27th, 2010, Spain will award Uribe "The Door of Memory" ("La Puerta del Recuerdo") award for his work toward the "coexistence of all Colombians" and his persistent work in the war on terror "by means of the strict application of the Law" and his "personal and political commitment" to the victims of terrorism.[86]

Uribe's DSDP aimed to do the following:

(1) gradually restore police presence in all municipalities;
(2) increase judicial action against crimes of high social impact;
(3) strengthen public institutions;
(4) reduce human rights violations;
(5) dismantle terrorist organizations;
(6) reduce kidnappings and extortion;
(7) reduce homicide levels;
(8) prevent forced displacement and facilitating the return of forcefully-displaced people; and
(9) continue to fight the illegal drug trade through interdiction, eradication, and judicial action.

The policy aimed to accomplish these goals by means of the following methods:

(1) engaging the civilian population more actively;
(2) supporting soldiers;
(3) increasing intelligence capacity;
(4) reinstating control over national roads;
(5) demobilizing illegal groups;
(6) integrating the armed forces services; and
(7) increasing defense spending.[87]

In the history of Colombia, no one had been more determined, better funded, and better equipped to fight the FARC and narco-terrorism than Uribe.

Some of Uribe's DSDP's major successes are found in the areas of reducing violence, strengthening the country's military apparatus, and weakening illegally armed groups. Though Uribe failed in ending the guerrillas once and for all, he did strike a blow to previous threats. In a February 2010 interview with Edgardo Buscaglia, the UN advisor on corruption and organized crime stated that Colombian mafia and drug cartels were no longer the biggest in the world and were far below the top three mafias. Buscaglia attributed this dramatic change to Uribe's DSDP.[88] FARC numbers alone were said to have been cut from 18,000 to 6,000 (low estimate) and the ELN was reduced to a fifth of its size to only 500 members, while 31,000 paramilitaries were said to have demobilized. Kidnapping decreased from 2,986 cases in 2002 to 213 in 2009 and terrorist acts decreased from 1,645 cases in 2002 to 387 cases in 2007. Even conditions for union members improved. For example, during Uribe's first term, assassinations, disappearances, detentions, kidnapping, torture, and displacement against union members decreased.[89] Further, when Uribe took office, Colombia produced 90 percent of the world's cocaine, which has been reduced to 50 percent.[90] Over the course of Uribe's tenure, foreign investment increased by 50 percent and the country experienced an average annual economic growth of 4 percent. This could not have occurred without some ability to promise investors security. The Joint Industrial Opinion Survey (EOIC), for example, concluded that insecurity problems declined under Uribe.[91] According to Uribe himself, in June of 2010, the Colombian state had finally achieved a monopoly of violence throughout the entire territory of Colombia.[92]

The U.S. recognizes that much of this success can be attributed to PC.

> Since Plan Colombia began in 2000, the U.S. Government has assisted Colombia with a comprehensive strategy to attack the growth and distribution of cocaine and heroin from Colombia. Eradication, interdiction and organizational attack have succeeded in creating the stability and security for alternative development, judicial reform, and the establishment of democratic institutions, effectively expanding the State's authority into areas previously controlled by criminal narco-terrorist groups.[93]

Further, as reported by the U.S. Office of National Drug Control Policy, since Uribe took office, there is now police presence in every single Colombian municipality (1,099), there has been an increase in road and highway security, homicides had "decreased by 40 percent, kidnappings by 83 percent, terrorist attacks by 76 percent, and attacks against the country's infrastructure by 60 percent."[94] However, as an unfortunate consequence, the internal conflict spilled across Colombia's borders, thereby displacing refugees, violence, and drug production and trafficking.

Uribe's campaign slogan when he first ran for the 2002 Colombian presidency was "Hard Fist, Big Heart"—a balance between consent and force. Uribe was to bring peace to Colombia by securing the lives of his citizens while simultaneously winning over the hearts and minds of Colombians. Putting an end to the covert world grounded Uribe's security strategy. While in office, however, his hard-lined, political realist attitude disposed his administrations to focus more on their hard fists over their supposed big hearts. As a result, Uribe's administrations realized an end-justify-the-means policy, thereby sacrificing the democratic of the DSDP for the security and defense aspects of the policy to attain and safeguard dominance. It was this disposition that gave rise to one of the gravest diplomatic crises and security dilemmas in the region's recent history.

PC's and the DSDP's domestic failures under Uribe

Before moving on to PC's and the DSDP's role in the Andean diplomatic crisis and security dilemma, let us first begin by outlining some of the major domestic failures of these policies to illustrate how both Uribe administrations sacrificed the democratic aspect of these strategies for the sake of security and defense. Though hailed as overwhelming successes, PC and the DSDP, under Uribe, violated many of the liberties and virtues they claimed to be working to uphold. Domestically, the main four can be identified as extrajudicial executions at the hands of the Colombian Armed Forces, Uribe's failure to prevent forced displacement and to facilitate the return of forcefully displaced persons, violations of civil liberties through the state's Administrative Department of Security

(DAS), and the persecution of victims of the armed conflict while victimizers were rewarded by means of Uribe's policies.

Extrajudicial executions

Civilian blood on the hands of Colombian security forces rose during Uribe's tenure.[95] The modernization of the military did not yield security in this regard since it was actually worse than the guerrillas in violating basic democratic and civil rights. The false positives scandal implicating Colombia's security forces is a prime example. Here we have a situation where extrajudicial executions of civilians—dressed up as rebel fighters—took place to increase body count in combat.[96] Philip Alston, UN special rapporteur, defined it as "cold-blooded, premeditated murder of innocent civilians for profit."[97] In April 2009, an internal investigation by the military concluded that the Colombian army compensated military personnel for every false positive presented as a rebel killed in combat. Such a reward system was issued back on November 17th of 2005 and recognized as Directive 029.[98] The motivation of Directive 029 was to provide the results Uribe demanded. The UN blamed the reward system for the extreme rise in extrajudicial executions at the hands of the country's security forces.[99]

The government's position that the assassinations were carried out only by a few bad apples and on a small scale—as Coronel Gabriel Pinilla stated, "It is very clear that these types of episodes have been isolated cases"[100]—is difficult to accept since the killings have been widespread and systematic. In fact, many charged with involvement in the false positives scandal were actually promoted after their deeds.[101] Reports by the Coordinación Colombia Europa Estados Unidos (CCEEU) claimed that extrajudicial killings were reported in 27 of the 32 departments—rising 67 percent from the time Uribe took office.[102] There were even reports of army officials going to Medellín streets to kill homeless persons to up the body count.[103] As the United Nations High Commissioner for Human Rights stated in October of 2008, "An offense becomes a crime against humanity if it is widespread and systematic against the civilian population. [...] We are observing and keeping a record of the number of extrajudicial killings, and it does appear systematic and widespread by my view,"[104] which under international humanitarian law international courts could intervene if the Colombian government was "unwilling or unable" to handle the investigations itself.[105]

Since the scandal broke out in the media in October of 2008, reported incidents of false positives have greatly been reduced and Directive 029 has been revised, though Uribe would not provide information on the changes. Nevertheless, investigations suggest that 3,796 civilians became false positives since 1994, 81 percent of them between 2002 and 2009.[106] Further investigations found an "alarming link" between armed forces units committing extrajudicial executions and those funded by the U.S.[107] It is not surprising that during the first seven years of Uribe's presidency Colombia was one of only two countries declaring it would not accept the International Criminal Court's (ICC) jurisdiction with respect to war crimes committed by Colombian nationals or such crimes enacted on Colombian soil, under Article 124.[108]

Uribe's actions and rhetoric made it clear he only wanted punishment to be ruled against the guerrillas and opposition, not for crimes enacted by paramilitaries, his administration, and Uribistas. For example, when, in June of 2010, Colonel Alfonso Plazas Vega was found guilty of forced civilian disappearances during the 1985 army siege of the Palace of Justice, Uribe's response demonstrated he would support his military even if its members too committed the same terrorist acts as the guerrillas. Uribe and the Ministry of Defense (Santos no longer a member) expressed their

> deep sorrow for the consequences of the court ruling that sentenced a soldier of the homeland. This painful and sad feeling is shared at all levels amongst ground, air, and sea soldiers, and their families. [The Ministry]

> manifests in these difficult times its solidarity with the
> Colonel Alfonso Plazas Vega and his respected family.[109]

What kind of commitment to defending democracy, reconciliation, and justice is there with a policy that rejects democratic principles and civil rights to ensure security and defense? Uribe publicly addressed the colonel's ruling, criticized the court, and sided with the colonel, claiming that "the way to support the victims of the Palace of Justice was not by making victims of the armed forces."[110] What kind of justice was Uribe promoting when a victimizer is recognized as the victim? Because of this case, Uribe suggested the military should only be tried by a military tribunal when it came to crimes against humanity. What exactly was the democracy about which Uribe spoke so eloquently when his words and actions dictated he and his military apparatus were above the law? Such a defense comes to no surprise when we recognize Uribe was the only president in the world to publicly express support and sympathy with the coup leaders who overthrew a democratically elected Honduran government in June of 2009.

Failure to prevent forced displacement and facilitate the return of forcefully displaced persons

Though the prevention of forced displacement and facilitation of returning forcefully displaced persons to their lands were two of the DSDP's main objectives, the militarization of the country failed immensely in this regard under Uribe. Almost 4.9-million Colombians—over 10 percent of the country's population and 19 percent of the world's internal refugees— have been forcibly displaced over the past 25 years, making it the second worst case in the world after the Sudan crisis.[111] In the last eight years alone, during Uribe's keep, 2.4 million Colombians were displaced. That is to say, more persons were disproportionately displaced during the exercise of Uribe's policy and at a faster rate.[112] According to Constitutional Court magistrate Luis Ernesto Vargas, the vast displacement has occurred not only because of the armed conflict, but also because the number of mega projects handed out by the Uribe administration (part of Uribe's investment "Virtuous Circle") to multi-nationals and corporations without first consulting local populations, such as the indigenous and Afro-Colombian communities.[113] These figures are difficult to comprehend when, according to Uribe's government rhetoric, paramilitaries ceased to exist and the FARC were nearing extinction, as General Freddy Padilla would often profess.

The objective of the forcible displacement of persons in Colombia is politically and economically motivated. Millions of hectares have been appropriated illegally, mostly by the government and government-allied paramilitaries, to use the land, exploit its resources, and enter the products into the global market.[114] The cultivation of African palm oil, for example, has made Colombia the second largest producer of the product in the world. Further, much of PC's funding was directed to areas of Colombia where new reserves of petroleum were discovered. Jorge Rojas, director of Consultancy for Human Rights and Displacement (CODHES),[115] claimed there is a direct correlation between the industry and displacement: "In almost every case where there is a big palm-oil development, there is widespread forced displacement."[116]

However, despite the UN and numerous human rights groups denouncing Colombian biofuel because its production is directly connected to systematic and widespread violations of human rights, the Uribe administration continued its public bewitchment of intellect by claiming, like Colombia Agriculture Minister Andres Fernandez did in 2009, the following: "I think that that is just a fallacy disseminated by people who don't believe in biofuels."[117] As with other human rights violation accusations against the Uribe government, the administration found a way to sidestep taking the issue seriously and denounced those who held such opposing views against government policy as terrorist, terrorist sympathizers, or rumor generators who wanted the government to fail and did not believe in its democracy. The dire refugee situation was overly neglected by both Uribe administrations. In July of 2008, for example, Uribe's former adviser, Jose Obdulio Gaviria, claimed there was no refugee or internal displacement in Colombia, but, instead, many migrant workers.[118] It is almost impossible to prevent forced displacement and facilitate the return of refugees if the state is in denial that such persons exist.

Violations of civil liberties by the state's Administrative Department of Security (DAS)

Surveillance and intelligence gathering were important goals of the DSDP. Colombia's DAS, however, which operated under the direct authority of Uribe, has been tied to a scandal labelled a political warfare by some and "worse than Watergate" by others. For example, a June 2010 report carried out by the Washington Office on Latin America, U.S. Office on Colombia, Latin America Working Group, and the Center for International Policy assessed that the scandal

> is even more shocking than initially reported, with the presidential intelligence agency, DAS, not only spying, but also carrying out dirty tricks and even death threats on major players in Colombia's democracy. [...][O]perations did not target alleged terrorists, but rather people carrying out legitimate, democratic activities, including: Supreme Court and Constitutional Court judges, presidential candidates, journalists, publishers, the Inter-American Commission on Human Rights, the United Nations and human rights defenders in Colombia, the United States, and Europe.[119]

DAS illegally intercepted communication for at least seven years, all during Uribe's tenure, and was implicated in colluding with paramilitaries.

What is also worrisome, according to the Colombian Attorney General's office, is the evidence linking Uribe, his private secretary, his Vice President, the former intelligence directors of DAS, former DAS officials, and other high-level officials in ordering wiretaps and death threats or knowing about them and doing nothing, or both. Former director, Jorge Noguera, for example, was charged with homicide and being a paramilitary himself. Noguera provided paramilitary groups information of trade union leaders, "several individuals named on the list were killed, threatened, or were reportedly the subject of arbitrary judicial proceedings."[120] Uribe had to dismantle the organization due to domestic and international pressure. The scandal, which broke out in 2009, forced Interpol to stop cooperating with DAS, thereby transferring cooperation to Colombia's National Police for intelligence. The U.S. Congress even demanded any U.S. financial assistance to DAS be stopped.

As of October 6th of 2010, Uribe's former Secretary General, two former DAS Directors, two former DAS Deputy Directors, and Uribe's Financial Intelligence Chief have been barred from holding public office for 18 to 20 years by Colombia's Inspector General for their roles in ordering illegal wiretaps. Though Uribe has always insisted he knew nothing about such crimes, on October 5th of 2010, Uribe assumed "judicial and political responsibility" for the conduct of his former Secretary General's role in the matter and stated he would make himself available for investigations.

Uribe's policies persecuted the victims and rewarded the victimizers

The justice and peace process so long cheered by the U.S. and Uribe for the so-called demobilization of 31,000 paramilitaries has fallen quite short of what was originally promised when Uribe instated the Justice and Peace Law 975 (2005), which was to be an instrumental component for achieving one of the DSDP's goal to increase judicial action against crimes of high social impact and strengthen public institutions. It was this law that allowed Uribe's administration to claim that in Colombia paramilitarism was extinct and identified those who argued otherwise as trying to undermine the successes of the DSDP.

This is exactly what Defense Minister Gabriel Silva claimed[121] in February 2010 after Human Rights Watch came out with a 122-page report, titled "Paramilitaries' Heirs: The New Face of Violence in Colombia," whose findings concluded that Uribe had "failed to treat the rise of successor groups with the seriousness the problem requires."[122] The report documented the "widespread and serious abuses" of the neo-paramilitaries.

The successes of the Justice and Peace Law, along with Uribe's DSDP and PC, continued to be overstated. The government claimed that 35,000 of total terrorists who had demobilized could be found working and studying.[123] Yet, non-governmental studies kept contradicting government figures. For example, Amnesty International's annual report on Colombia concluded that

> [o]nly around 3,700 of the 31,000 paramilitaries who had allegedly demobilized since 2003 had participated in the Justice and Peace process by the end of 2009. However, the whereabouts of many of these were unknown. [...] Some 90 per cent of those who were demobilized continued to escape effective investigation as a result of Decree 128 and Law 782, which grant de facto amnesties to those not under investigation for human rights violations. In June, congress approved a law to regularize the legal status of 19,000 supposedly demobilized paramilitaries after the Supreme Court ruled in 2008 that they could not benefit from amnesties. The law authorized the Attorney General to suspend, interrupt or abandon investigations against them, thus enabling them to evade justice. [...] By the end of the year, no paramilitary had been sentenced under the Justice Peace process.[124]

Such findings suggest that the promises of the law have not materialized.

The purpose of the Justice and Peace Law, however, was not only to demobilize terrorists for the sake of peace, but also to balance the scale of justice. Repairing victims supposed to be one of the main aspects of the process but was also a failure. For starters, the first ever hearing held between both victims and paramilitaries occurred in April of 2010, a whole seven years after demobilization commenced and five years after Congress approved the law.[125] The National Reparation and Reconciliation Commission (NRRC) even declared that reparations to victims had been "absolutely insufficient." The Commission's head, Eduardo Pizarro, was very critical of the process and said the problem with the Justice and Peace Law was that

> [i]t doesn't say when they [paramilitaries] should deliver the reparations, and the Supreme Court hasn't said either. If you ask me what is the main reason for this, it is because of legal loopholes. They left open the possibility for them to give reparations after their sentences ... [allowing them to] take advantage of five years of making the resources disappear, to sell everything and hide their tracks. [...] Also, they are selling their resources to honest buyers, and to take away [from those honest buyers] what they bought is something virtually legally impossible. We gave them [the paramilitaries] a gift: five years to make their resources disappear.[126]

Pizarro elaborated on the fact that there is new violence against the victims who were trying to reclaim the lands they lost through forced displacement. On a different level, after the main paramilitary leaders were jailed and later extradited to the U.S., Pizarro added that "their deputies, front men, and mid-level leaders [were forced] to wage war against each other and those threatening their ownership to the land deeds."[127]

This land-grab fight had further impact in damaging the progress of the Justice and Peace Law. Primo Levi's claim that much of today's violence stems from the violence of the past[128] seems to explain Colombia's situation. Many victims who can apply for reparations do not because, as Corporación Arco Iris (Colombian think-tank) explained, they either do not know they can or "the presence of armed groups impedes their mobility." Many have been assassinated or had their lives threatened, which keeps them from registering as victims or making claims. By April 2010, the Ministry of Interior had received almost 1,500 requests for protection, of which only 214 were granted. According to Corporación Arco Iris, of victims eligible to file a claim, around 60 percent have not. This is a staggering figure since according to a report by the Justice and Peace unit of the Prosecutor General's Office, as of April 2010, 305,957 victims had registered and sought reparations. From these claims, over 200,000 sought reparations for assassinations, about 30,000 for forced disappearances, and some 10,000 for being kidnapped. Since demobilization began, only 10,500 claims for reparations (as of April 2010) had been approved. Sadly, because the government denies the existence of paramilitary groups, victims of the conflict ran out of time in April of 2010 to submit a claim for reparations. Thus, most of the victims of the recent armed conflict have not only *not* been repaired but will not be able to. Yet, extra-judicial executions, forced displacement, torture, kidnapping, disappearances, etc., continue at the hands of neo-paramilitaries, guerrillas, narco-traffickers, and, probably even more unfortunately, the Colombian Armed Forces. As Pizarro suggested, the deadline for filing claims should be lifted indefinitely until the cycle of violence is over.[129]

In addition, most of the paramilitary warlords, responsible for tens of thousands of assassinations, would not be tried for crimes against humanity, but, instead, were extradited to the U.S. to be tried for narco-trafficking, and, in accordance with a deal made with the Uribe administration, would receive up to eight years in prison if found guilty. As Jasmin Hristov suggested in *Blood and Capital: The Paramilitarization of Colombia*, Uribe's negotiation with the paramilitaries looked more like a legalization of the paramilitaries and not a sincere demobilization effort.[130] Further, civil society—the real victims of the conflict—was excluded from negotiations with the paramilitaries.[131] In fact, though on paper and abroad Uribe publicly recognized the paramilitaries as terrorists, his administration time and again tried to justify their crimes, accommodate them, and even did its best to pardon all paramilitary crimes—such as through Decree 128 of 2003. Hristov was correct to point out that one major flaw of the Justice and Peace Law was the "failure to consider the rights of victims to truth, justice, and reparation." She further recognized, like many others, that a roadblock for the country's reconciliation process—along with establishing justice and truth gathering—was Uribe's decision to not set a date, or goal, for establishing some form of history that chronicled the nation's violence (at the hands of the state, paramilitaries, guerrillas, etc.).

Hristov's concern is a key element for the country to be able to move forward with the reconciliation process, which is so important for individuals to start the healing process.[132] Fortunately, at the hands of the judiciary—one of the few institutions Uribe was not able to fully control—some of the focus has been redirected from punishing victimizers to dealing with the concerns of the victims. In June, the Ministry of Justice, after many complaints of Uribe's extradition practices and the court's denying the extradition of other paramilitary bosses, the law was amended through decree 2288 of June 25th, 2010. Now, a demobilized paramilitary must meet with the process of national reparation *before* being extradited. This means crimes against humanity will finally start taking a priority over drug trafficking.[133] Though Uribe claimed his government did the best it could to ensure the participation of the paramilitaries in the justice and peace process, those very same paramilitaries often complained that their extradition actually impeded their participation.[134]

Further, public institutions essential for conflict resolution and reconciliation were under-funded by Uribe's government, demonstrating that it was more concerned with modernizing its military apparatus, securing capital investment, and

111

defeating the FARC. For example, in April of 2010, the Colombian Prosecutor General's Office confirmed 300,000 official registered complaints against paramilitaries, including 157,000 extrajudicial executions to which 32,000 assassinations the paramilitaries had already confessed.[135] However, on August 24th of 2010, the same office expressed it did not have a budget and "sufficient resources" to investigate the large number of complaints, of which only 7 percent had been investigated.[136] Uribe's policies failed millions by persecuting the victims and rewarding the victimizers.

The Regionalization of Colombia's Armed Conflict

PC was instrumental in Uribe's DSDP, which are considered responsible for saving Colombia from becoming a failed state. Nevertheless, as elaborated above, PC and the DSDP can also be blamed for many crimes against humanity, human rights violations, and a disregard for the concerns of the country's most vulnerable populations. PC and the DSDP, as enacted by Uribe, are also responsible for provoking conflict with Colombia's neighbors. In this section, I unpack Uribe's DSDP and its negative impact on the Andes region. The main regional tensions I highlight are the spill-over effect of Colombia's armed conflict (e.g., violence, refugees, drug production, and narco-trafficking); the March 1st, 2008, raid of a FARC camp on Ecuadorian territory; the August 2009 U.S.-Colombian military base agreement; and the apparent tolerance of Ecuador and Venezuela of the FARC.

Displacement of Colombia's armed conflict in the Andes

According to María Camila López Rojas, in her article "Effects of the Regionalization of the Democratic Security Policy: Upon Displacement at Colombia's Borders," the DSDP, along with PC, may have been partially effective for regaining national control of the monopoly of violence and re-establishing a semblance of authority throughout Colombian territory, but also had dire implications for the region. For example, large numbers of forcibly displaced persons within Colombia's borders and across them, especially to neighboring Ecuador and Venezuela, resulted from PC and the DSDP under Uribe. She criticized the Uribe government for not having "legal and institutional support [...] that could guarantee human rights protection under its immigrant condition."[137] According to CODHES, the Colombian displaced persons issue has impacted Ecuador, Panama, and Venezuela in similar ways.

In 2006, for example, 5,301 Colombians applied for asylum in Ecuador, Panama, and Venezuela because they were caught in the middle of the armed conflict and, in turn, were displaced.[138] Between 2002 and 2006, during Uribe's first presidential term, almost 40,500 Colombian refugees requested asylum in Ecuador alone.[139] For this reason, the UN's largest refugee agency in the hemisphere (UNHCR) is located on the border between Colombia and Ecuador in Lago Agrio, Ecuador. As stated earlier, from 2002 to 2010, during Uribe's keep, 2.4 million Colombians were internally displaced because of the armed conflict. That is to say, more persons were displaced during the exercise of Uribe's policies and at a faster rate than previous years and decades.[140] Further, a January 2010 study conducted by Ibernet Media & Consultants concluded that as of December 2009, there were 5.5 million Colombians living abroad, while over a third of this figure migrated after Uribe took office.[141] In 2009, the UN estimated that some 3 to 4 million Colombians were living in Venezuela, of which 200,000 were war refugees that had crossed the border from Colombia.[142]

Since Uribe took office, his U.S.-supported all-out war against insurgents has pushed the armed conflict closer to the outskirts of the country, thereby spilling over into neighboring states. The fighting between the armed forces, paramilitaries, guerrillas, along with common delinquency and drug trafficking crossing the borders—mostly into Ecuador since this is where most of the war on narco-terrorism is being fought in southern Colombia—violence and insecurity has been on the rise. Due to the Colombian conflict being pushed to the Ecuadorian-Colombian border, Ecuador's military budget had to be increased by 40% and police budget by 30%. From the first year of the DSDP through the end of Uribe's first term, Ecuador had to triple the amount of armed forces on the border.[143] Ecuadorian Defense Minister, Javier Ponce Cevallos, has asked the U.S. to do more to help Colombia secure the Colombia-Ecuador border since the spill-over effect of PC and the DSDP has put a strain on Ecuador's limited resources. Ecuador has had to spend $100 million annually to secure the area. The Ecuadorian government estimates that about 140,000 Colombian refugees have crossed the border, which the Ecuadorian government now must regulate more intensely by sending 10,000 troops to the area (about a third of Ecuador's military members). Uribe did not aid these refugees, which further strained relations with neighbors since they had to create budgets to deal with Colombia's displaced armed conflict. A similar situation is occurring along the Colombia-Venezuela border, as residents constantly complain of onslaughts from the guerrillas and paramilitaries and consider themselves "victim[s] of illegal Colombian groups." Though these border towns have had to deal with the spill-over of Colombia's armed conflict for decades, residents claim the problem has worsened in recent times.[144]

Further, along with refugees and violence, production and trafficking of illicit drugs were also displaced. Like stated earlier, since PC's implementation, the U.S. and the Colombian government have deemed successful one of the DSDP's goals—to continue to fight illegal drug trade through interdiction, eradication, and judicial action. The U.S. and Colombia praise their policies for reducing Colombia's international status as being the world's number one producer of cocaine. When Uribe became president, Colombia produced roughly 90 percent of the illicit drug, but by the end of his second term that figure had dropped to around 50%. By some estimates, Colombia is no longer the world's leading cocaine producer, as Peru seems to be retaking the infamous spot. The issue, however, is with hailing U.S. and Colombian efforts as overwhelming successes since what appears to have occurred is not the elimination of the illegal drug trade, but its displacement to other Andean nations, like Peru. Furthermore, PC has failed to reduce the availability or use of cocaine in the U.S.

The U.S.-Colombia decision to fight the production at the source while disregarding focus on the consumers of the illicit drugs has also produced efforts that have further strained already fragile relations. Colombia is currently the only country in the world using aerial fumigation to eradicate illicit crops. This method has also had spill-over effects in northern Ecuador. The inability for Ecuador and Colombia, under Uribe, to diplomatically negotiate Ecuador's concerns with the aerial fumigation led Ecuador to issue a proceeding against Colombia at the International Court of Justice. Ecuador claims that Colombia's actions have "caused serious damage to people, to crops, to animals, and to the natural environment on the Ecuadorian side of the frontier."[145] Despite such pressures and resistance against PC's aerial fumigation strategy, Colombia decided in March of 2009 to follow the same policy, but this time in Colombia's northern border with Venezuela.[146]

Roots of the Andean diplomatic crisis and security dilemma

2008: Colombian military incursion

Though these three issues of displacement—refugees, violence, and the illicit drug trade—have caused tensions between Colombia and its neighbors in the twenty-first century, it was not until Colombia's actions on March 1st of 2008, fully supported by the U.S., that the disputes escalated into a near armed confrontation between states in the region. Colombia's decision to bomb a FARC camp housing alias Raúl Reyes (Luis Edgar Devia Silva)—then the FARC's second most important guerrilla leader—on Ecuadorian soil, unilaterally, without collaborating with or informing Ecuadorian authorities, sparked the fire that set the Andean diplomatic crisis and security dilemma ablaze.

The incursion—whose casualties included mostly FARC guerrillas, but also an Ecuadorian national and wounded a few Mexican students—led both Ecuador and Venezuela to send troops to their borders with Colombia. Conversely, Colombia decided against mobilizing troops to the borders, but did so internally anticipating a possible FARC retaliation. Ecuador and Venezuela also removed their ambassadors from Colombia and expelled Colombian ambassadors from their countries, and Venezuela restricted traffic along the Colombian border. The diplomatic and security crisis had begun.

Though the Colombian government initially claimed the bombing occurred as Colombian Armed Forces were in hot pursuit of guerrilla fighters in the jungle, soon thereafter it was revealed the incursion was planned and assisted by the U.S. FBI and DEA.[147] Ecuador considered the incursion a violation of Ecuadorian air space, territorial sovereignty, Ecuadorian law, and international law. Venezuela denounced the raid and expressed its fears of the operation being part of a greater U.S. plot to destabilize the region. The Organization of America States agreed that the Colombian raid was a violation of Ecuadorian sovereignty, but did not condemn the operation.[148]

Colombia apologized for its hot pursuit but justified the incursion on the basis that Ecuador was known for harboring FARC guerrillas. As Juan Manuel Santos, then Colombian Defense Minister, stated, "If we had real collaboration from Ecuador in pursuing these groups, these situations wouldn't occur, but we've never had it. They always have taken the position that they do not want to interfere in the Colombian conflict."[149] When I spoke with U.S. Consulate General Phillip Chicola about the incident, he expressed how thorny the situation was. Chicola admitted the operation was illegal under international law, but suggested it was justifiable considering Ecuador's role in harboring terrorists. Chicola informed me that in 1999 he met with Raúl Reyes in Costa Rica as part of an attempt by the U.S. to aid in peace negotiations between the FARC and the Colombian government. Chicola claimed Reyes had to postpone their meeting several times because, as Chicola paraphrased Reyes's excuse, it took months for the FARC to buy off the Ecuadorian security forces at the border to leave Colombia and make the meeting.[150]

From the camp, Colombian officials claimed to have retrieved laptops and documents that connected both Ecuadorian and Venezuelan governments to the FARC. Ecuador insisted that such evidence be shared to verify the information. Though Uribe's administration promised it would do so, it never did, causing further complications. Although it appeared that Colombia, Ecuador, and Venezuela made peace on March 7th of 2008 during the emergency Rio Group summit in Santo Domingo, Dominican Republic, security, diplomatic, and trade disputes continued and were never to return to normalcy for the remaining two and a half years of Uribe's final presidential term. For the remainder of Uribe's tenure, the crisis damaged trade relations between Venezuela and Colombia, costing the two nations billions of dollars, which were directly tied to higher unemployment figures in both countries—Colombia's being the worst in the hemisphere. For example, bilateral trade was down 73 percent during the first quarter of 2010 between Colombia and Venezuela in comparison to the same period the previous year. In July of 2010, Uribe stated that if it were not for the world economic crisis and the crisis with Venezuela, unemployment would have been at 9 percent instead of 12.1 percent.[151] Tensions between Colombia, Ecuador, and Venezuela waxed and waned continually through August of

2009 when the region's second major diplomatic and security crisis spiked.

2009: U.S.-Colombia Military Agreement

Knowing that Ecuadorian President Rafael Correa was not going to renew the U.S. Manta military instillation in Ecuador, the U.S. began negotiations for a similar military agreement with Colombia. Considering the recent crisis in the region, South American countries were concerned about the motivation of the possible pact and if it would be used by Colombia and the U.S. in unilateral military missions, like the Ecuadorian incursion of 2008, or for surveillance and spying operations. Since the U.S. and Colombia would not disclose information about the military agreement, the situation was cause for alarm, and another set of emergency meetings, this time starting with the Union of South American Nations (UNASUR) in Bariloche, Argentina, on August 28th of 2009.

The Bariloche emergency summit of South American presidents ended with a call for peace in the region. The organization concluded that "the presence of foreign military forces cannot, with its means and linked resources to goals, threaten the sovereignty and integrity of any South American nations and, in consequence, the peace and security of the region." In doing so, UNASUR agreed "to establish a mechanism of mutual trust regarding defense and security" in South America. Colombia defended the military agreement by claiming it would not be providing the U.S. with military bases, but that the U.S. would have access to Colombian bases to help Colombia fight narco-terrorism within the country's borders. Nevertheless, Uribe's statement was not reassuring for many UNASUR members, especially Bolivian President Evo Morales, who proposed that South America should unite to not grant foreign nations military bases, or access to them. Venezuelan President Hugo Chávez considered the agreement a threat, especially since the U.S. had previously supported a failed coup attempt against him and Venezuela in April of

2002. Chávez considered the agreement a "war policy" that "could generate a war in South America." Others, like Peru's Alan Garcia and Brazil's Luis Inácio Lula da Silva, were satisfied with the agreement if there could be some transparent guarantee that U.S.-Colombia operations would be restricted to Colombian territory and would not cross that nation's border. Argentine President Cristina Fernandez suggested the UNASUR Defense Council review the U.S.-Colombian military pact, but Uribe countered by removing that option from the table of possibilities since the agreement was already decided upon and would not be reconsidered.

Though the Bariloche summit seemed to at least calm tensions for a little while, a leaked U.S. Air Force document further complicated matters. According to this original May 2009 document,

> [e]stablishing a Cooperative Security Location (CSL) in Palanquero best supports the COCOM's (Command Combatant's) Theater Posture Strategy and demonstrates our commitment to this relationship. Development of this CSL provides a unique opportunity for full spectrum operations in a critical sub-region of our hemisphere where security and stability is under constant threat from narcotics funded terrorist insurgencies, anti-US governments, endemic poverty and recurring natural disasters. [...] Palenquero is unquestionably the best site for investing in infrastructure development within Colombia. Its central location is within reach of operation areas, its isolation maximizes Operational Security (OPSEC) and Force Protection and minimizes the US military profile. The intent is to leverage existing infrastructure to the maximum extent possible, improve the US ability to respond rapidly to crisis, and assure regional access and presence at minimum cost. Palanquero supports the mobility mission by providing access to the entire South American continent with the exception of Cape Horn. [...] Development of this CSL will further the strategic partnership forged between the US and Colombia and is in the interest of both nations. [...] A presence will also increase our capability to conduct Intelligence,

> Surveillance and Reconnaissance (ISR), improve global
> reach, support logistics requirements, improve
> partnerships, improve theater security cooperation and
> expand expeditionary warfare capability.[152]

Though after being leaked the document was later modified, on November 16th of 2009,[153] so the U.S. did not look like it was interested in South America as a whole, the leaked document illustrated to South American nations U.S. intentions and why both Colombia and the U.S. were so hesitant to be transparent about the military agreement.

The actual agreement was finally signed on October 30th of 2009. Colombia granted the U.S. the use of seven Colombian military bases, airports, and unlimited use of Colombian territory for military operations. Though Uribe's administration consistently claimed that the U.S.-Colombian military agreement was only an extension of a previous 1974 military agreement with the U.S. and not a new pact, the region continued to be concerned. Those who felt most threatened by the agreement were Bolivia, Ecuador, and Venezuela because Washington considers their administrations to be against U.S. interests. The fears, of course, were another incursion, a war, or a coup attempt, which, coincidentally, just occurred in Ecuador in late September 2010. Uribe's disregard for the concerns of its neighbors did not help rebuild diplomatic and economic ties with Ecuador and Venezuela, as they continued to follow a similar pattern that was started on March 1st of 2008.

2010: 'Harboring terrorists' allegations

Uribe's own concerns did not end with the signing of the U.S. military pact, however. Uribe's administration decided to press Venezuela with further allegations of new evidence that Venezuela had harbored Colombian guerrilla camps. The U.S. supported Colombia claiming that they had been "concerned about this for some time and it's one of the reasons why, since 2006, Venezuela has been judged not to be fully cooperating on anti-terrorism efforts."[154] Venezuela responded to the allegations with, again, breaking off total diplomatic and trade ties with Colombia, mobilized military troops to the Colombian border in preparation for war, while threatening to cut off the U.S. from Venezuelan oil exports if they started a war. Others, like Bolivian President Evo Morales, called for another emergency UNASUR summit because, as he saw it, "A war is in the making and Bolivia, along with the presidents of the UNASUR, should not allow that war to happen between brother countries."[155] Uribe denied any charge that Colombia was on a war path, but for the next two and a half weeks tension in the region continued and was expected to continue after Uribe stepped down from the presidency on August 7th of 2010.

Santos diffuses the Andean diplomatic crisis and security dilemma

As Uribe's chosen heir to his throne; as his former Minister of Defense during the Ecuadorian incursion and the false positives scandal; as a presidential candidate who did not regret his March 1st of 2008 decisions but was proud of them and would commit them again if the situation would ever present itself; and as a man against whom Ecuador issued an arrest warrant due to his involvement in the incursion, Juan Manuel Santos was inaugurated Colombia's new President on August 7th of 2010. With such a track record behind him and close ties to Uribe's security and defense policies, many were under the impression that the Andean diplomatic crisis and security dilemma would continue long after Uribe, unwillingly, left power. Surprisingly, it turned out that Santos was not Uribe. Most political analysts and regional governments were shocked at the tremendous differences between the two politicians, especially when it came to reconciling with a resentful domestic population and concerned neighbors by taking their grievances seriously.

The change in domestic and foreign policies under Santos came at an opportune time. Though he continued with PC and the DSDP, he changed tactics to fulfill the goals outlined in both policies. For example, it appears the Santos administration took the recommendations from an unprecedented report, "Foreign Policy Mission," headed by a commission of local and foreign experts and former government officials.[156] Further, the changes Santos's administration has made and is pushing for with his domestic policy will also benefit the most vulnerable of the Colombian population. I have outlined some of these changes below.

- The current government and the Inter-American Institute of Human Rights signed a memorandum of understanding to improve the full respect of human rights and international humanitarian law in Colombia.[157]
- Santos launched a citizen feedback program that would aid in giving a voice to the masses by using twenty-first-century technology—especially the internet, cellular phones, and text messaging. In this way, citizens can better express opinions, critiques, and offer suggestions to the Santos administration.[158]
- Land reform has finally become a top priority for the Colombian government under Santos. The goal is to return illegally appropriated land to over 4 million Colombians or provide displaced persons with arable land as part of the country's new agricultural policy.[159]
- Santos has also committed to building one million new homes during the next four years.[160]
- On August 17th of 2010, ten days after Uribe left office, Colombia's Constitutional Court deemed the regionally feared military agreement with the U.S. "unconstitutional," that it was not just a mere extension of a previous pact, and, thus, it must first be submitted to Congress for approval.[161] The Santos

administration accepted the ruling without lashing out at the judiciary, like Uribe's government was accustomed when it did not like the ruling. This prompted a new relationship between the branches of government in that the Santos administration has made it a priority to abide by the judiciary's rulings.[162] As Interior and Justice Minister already stated, "one of the principles of this government is to not question judicial decisions."[163]

- Further, to ensure justice, reparations, and reconciliation, the Santos administration ratified legislation that would recognize victims of state crimes, which the Uribe government was against.[164]

Santos's foreign policy, which focuses on reconciliation, has received "unconditional support" from the country's foreign policy commission,[165] and has managed to also diffuse tensions with neighbors. The new policy would pay greater attention to "diplomacy, regional integration, the diversification of international relationships, cooperation, and human rights."[166] Below are some of the main results of Colombia's new foreign policy in the Andes region, which differed from the previous Uribe policy.

- Santos agreed to work with Ecuador and create a joint commission to deal with the Colombian refugee situation in Ecuador, long ignored by Uribe and, as a result, costly for Ecuador. Without Colombian assistance, Ecuador has been "obligated to finance the process of family reunification, and provide housing, food and general assistance until the refugees are able to live independently."[167] Ecuador's Vice Foreign Minister, Kintto Lucas, claimed on September 2nd of 2010 that Colombia was finally assuming the responsibility required to deal with the refugee situation.[168]

- On August 30th of 2010, Ecuadorian authorities

revoked its court's arrest warrant for Santos.[169]

- The Ecuador concern regarding aerial fumigation will be settled by the International Court of Justice in 2012.[170]

- On his inauguration day, one of the first things Santos did was hand over to Ecuadorian President Correa the laptop taken from Reyes's guerrilla camp on Ecuadorian territory after the March 1ˢᵗ of 2008 incursion. With this gesture, Santos expressed the political will Ecuador was looking for to begin to restore relations that had been broken for two and a half years. Ecuador had refused to restore diplomatic relations with Colombia until the laptop was handed over.[171]

- Ecuador has become confident that relations will be restored with Colombia before the end of the 2010 year because, as Ecuador's Vice Foreign Minister Kintto Lucas stated, Colombia has increased the "political will" to "address the solution of certain problems" that have long stood in the way of bilateral relations.[172]

- Colombia's and Ecuador's foreign ministers announced in late August 2010 that they would meet twice in October to address the long-standing diplomatic issue since the 2008 incursion. Santos and Correa are set to meet.[173]

- Considering regional concerns regarding the potential U.S.-Colombia military agreement, Santos, after the pact was considered unconstitutional by the Colombian judiciary, ensured the region that if Colombia decides to follow through with the pact via the legislature, the treaty would include transparent and explicit clauses that would not allow the U.S. to use Colombia as a base for South American surveillance, intelligence gathering, and military operations.[174]

- Similar meetings and bilateral commissions are

solidifying between Colombia and Venezuela. The two countries have decided to invest in their shared border to tackle narco-terrorism. They are also working on boosting tourism and the transport of energy resources across the border. President Santos and President Chávez are set to meet at the end of October 2010 to finalize the bilateral relations, which will be their second meeting since Santos became President.

- Venezuela has demobilized troops from its Colombian border, and trade and ambassadors have resumed their roles.

- The Santos administration also ceased pressing for an international investigation to verify the Uribe government's allegations that Venezuela was harboring terrorists. As Colombia's Foreign Minister, Maria Angela Holguin, stated, "Verification, no. We are looking forward. We are going to see in terms of security what mechanisms we can implement. The idea is that the security commission defines the best methods."[175] After the first Santos-Chávez summit in August 2010, relations were restored, and Chávez agreed to not tolerate guerrillas on Venezuelan territory. Originally, after the July 22nd of 2010 allegations, Colombia and the U.S. were in full support of the probes.

- Santos has also shown regional solidarity with two thorny topics: coups and the drug war. After the September 30th attempted coup in Ecuador, Santos closed Colombia's Ecuadorian border in solidarity with President Correa and sent him his full support. This was a change of tone from Uribe, who had publicly supported the Honduran coup of June 2009. Further, regarding the drug war, on August 25th of 2010, Santos supported Mexico's call for drug legalization and announced to create a "united stance with Mexico and Peru on the legalization issue" if California votes to legalize marijuana on November 2nd of 2010. As Santos put it, "How would we explain to an indigenous person on a Colombian mountain that producing marijuana is illegal and take him to jail, or destroy the marijuana, when in the U.S. it is legal to consume it?"[176]

- Further, there appears to be a shift with the Obama administration from previous presidencies and their disposition to the drug war. As U.S. Ambassador to Bogotá, Michael Mckinley, stated on October 7th of 2010, the U.S. recognizes that demand plays an important role in the narco-terrorism problem, and, thus, "the United States is focused on reduction in demand."[177] Also, Obama's new drug czar, Richard Gil Kerlikowske (since May 7th of 2009), has also pressed that PC needs to evolve into "a more balanced approach [which] can not only consist of repression through the judicial system or with soldiers. [...] We want to reduce the demand. We want to look at ways that help people to leave drugs and convert themselves into productive members of society."[178]

Though there is much left to be done to restore calm, security, diplomacy, trade, and to quiet the fires of resentment, the horizon in the Andes is the most tranquil it has been since the March 1st of 2008 incursion, when the crisis broke out like a wildfire. Much of the rhetoric and many of the policies supported by Santos have not been fully implemented, so we will have to re-evaluate the situation throughout his term. Nevertheless, it is safe to conclude that Santos more effectively positioned Colombia to realize the country's domestic and regional goals than Uribe ever did.

Now that I have discussed the main differences in governing between Uribe and Santos, in the concluding section I unpack and analyze why Uribe failed at diffusing the Andean diplomatic crisis and security dilemma and why Santos has so far succeeded by using Machiavellian and Gramscian political strategies as our interpretive lenses to understand how and why the crisis evolved the way it did.

Concluding thoughts: Marrying coercion and consent

Winning over the people and having an effective strategy was as important to Machiavelli as it was to Gramsci. Machiavelli, in *The Prince* and in *The Discourses* and Gramsci in *Selections from the Prison Notebooks* presented a more effective strategy for fulfilling self-interests without primarily focusing on force and coercion. They acknowledged that all humans have concerns and that it is more useful for a leader to achieve self-interests by simultaneously fulfilling public interest. In this way, by winning over the consent of the people and neighbors, entities can more effectively satisfy their concerns. If the head of state, for example, uses naked force to achieve self-interests, this spawns vengeance, rebellions, conspiracies, and revolution against leaders, thereby producing a constant state of fear, mistrust, and dissatisfaction that can destroy a state. Machiavelli and Gramsci proposed that winning over the hearts of the people and neighbors involves being an effective reader of the world. A leader must act accordingly to the drift of conditions to anticipate breakdowns, take care of obligations, and fulfill concerns satisfactorily. It is apparent that such advice was not heeded by former President Uribe but was taken to heart by President Santos. The growth and diffusion of the Andean diplomatic crisis and security dilemma since March 1st of 2010 are tributes to the relevance of Machiavellian and Gramscian strategies for effectively achieving state goals.

Machiavelli understood war to be caused by a desire or an act to subjugate others, or by fear of being subjugated.[179] War could also emerge from individuals or groups that determined they had been slighted and sought some form of revenge or retribution.[180] Such instances underscore the Andean diplomatic crisis and security dilemma. For this reason, a leader needs to treat subjects and neighbors with generosity and kindness so as not to fear rebellion or conspiracy, as Colombia and the region feared under Uribe.[181] A good way to redirect vengeance, hatred, and anger is to provide the people with an outlet, such as courts, where they may receive retribution and have their concerns taken seriously.[182] As Machiavelli indicated, "a prince need trouble little about conspiracies when the people are well disposed, but when they are hostile and hold him in hatred, then he must fear everything and everybody."[183] A significant portion of the Colombian population, illegally armed combatants and non-combatants alike, however, held Uribe in contempt for disregarding the concerns of Colombia's most vulnerable peoples: indigenous, Afro-Colombians, peasants, poor, women, children, forcibly displaced persons, and other victims of the armed conflict. This paved the way for a justifiable fear, on Uribe's part, of an internal and external threat and conspiracy, whose mission was to topple his government. States planning on attacking will benefit from re-evaluating their stance if the opposing state is united, which Colombia was not.[184] In turn, it is essential to not be hated by the populace or foreign states[185] since power is only lost when others are against you.[186] Though Uribe may have saved Colombia from becoming a failed state, the implementation of his DSDP, partially funded by PC, attracted many enemies along the way.

Being thoroughly aware of conditions and situations is needed when preparing to act accordingly. "[The leader] must have [a] mind disposed to adapt itself according to the wind," wrote Machiavelli, "and as the variations of fortune dictate."[187] This makes it imperative to take note of the governed and the desires and actions of foreigners at all times so as to be in touch with the times and react accordingly.[188] Being well versed in the nature of people helps take care of concerns effectively and helps to avoid detrimental risks since people react differently under different conditions.[189] For Machiavelli, people act according to love, fear, or hate.[190] Since every state is divided into two political economic parts, it is important to know what each part fears and desires so as to prepare more effectively for action.

According to Machiavelli, the political economy, divided between the haves and the have-nots, is what needs careful study.[191] The haves desire to dominate and keep their position in society, and are afraid of losing what they have.[192] On the other hand, the have-nots possess a great desire to not be dominated, want to acquire position, and wish to have more.[193] Keeping the populace happy should not be too difficult because essentially they just do not want to be oppressed or slighted.[194] In contrast, the masses will take up arms against tyrannies or unjustified force when consent, liberty, and free will are removed, challenged, or threatened.[195] When the people feel they have been wronged, they usually desire to regain their freedom and to "avenge themselves against the persons who have been the cause of their servitude."[196] Leaders must do what they can to achieve the best possible outcome for all sides of the political economy.

This rigorous preparation aids in constructing a solid foundation for a state; without this base the state is disposed for ruin.[197] "Since all our actions resemble those of nature," wrote Machiavelli, "it is neither possible nor natural that a slender trunk should support a heavy branch."[198] It is necessary for a leader to acquire the love, friendship, and consent of the people and neighbors to take care of the interests of all.[199] The people depend on the leader as much as the leader depends on the people. Both need one another to fulfill their respective concerns. In turn, satisfying the populace is one of the most important things a leader needs to do.[200] The people need to be well-disposed if the government wants anything done.[201] It is just as important when leading a state's subjects, as it is leading soldiers, to have their morale in good order since morale is directly tied to victory and achieving ends.[202] Similarly, in times of danger and adversity, if the state does not have the friendship and allegiance of the people and neighbors, then the decline of the state is more likely.[203] Without this support, enemies are sure to attack and have an easier time acquiring what they want.

It is difficult to eliminate a leader if he or she is loved[204] because if the conspirators are successful, they will have to deal with an angry mob.[205] As Machiavelli reasoned, "The best fortress is to be found in the love of the people, for although you may have fortresses they will not save you if you are hated by the people. When once the people have taken arms against you, there will never be lacking foreigners to assist them."[206] If people are supportive, all needed for security is internal forces.[207] Machiavelli explained that "A prince who fears his own people more than foreigners ought to build fortresses, but he who fears foreigners more than his own people ought to do without them."[208] Uribe feared both, which explained his obsession with militarizing Colombia. For this reason, the strength of a state should always be measured by the love of its people and its relationship to neighbors. A state is only as strong as its foundation, and the unity, confidence, and satisfaction of the people determines its strength.[209]

Security was of utmost importance for Machiavelli to fulfill interests, but it is how a state goes about achieving this that we must regard carefully. Security and the avoidance of war can be realized by a state if

> it be difficult to take by assault, owing to its being well organized for defense [...] rarely or never will it occur to anyone to seize it. And, if it be content with its own territory, and it becomes clear by experience that it has no ambitions, it will never occur that someone may make war through fear for himself, especially if by its constitution or by its laws expansion is prohibited. Nor have I the least doubt that, if this balance could be maintained, there would be genuine political life and real tranquility in such a city.[210]

It was clear Uribe—and the U.S., for that matter—was not content fulfilling his ambitions within the borders of his own territory. Further, he did not express sincere regret or remorse when the violence and illegal activities were displaced unto neighboring countries as a direct result of PC and the DSDP. An abundance of force and monetary wealth are never enough to secure a state.[211] Nevertheless, war is justified only as a last resort and if forced to it.[212] Such policies marginalized Colombia in the region, especially when it could not, under Uribe, gain the trust of neighbors nor convince them that their autonomy and sovereignty would not be violated again. Uribe lost consent in the region, which made it difficult for his administration to secure its interests as neighboring countries broke trade and diplomatic relations with Colombia, some even sent military troops and tanks to Colombia's borders. The Andean diplomatic crisis and security dilemma was an example of how a state can create a strong opposition and resistance when the love and consent of the people and neighbors are not effectively and sincerely considered and a state only acts on behalf of its own self-interests.

Antonio Gramsci, like Machiavelli, suggested hegemony did not have to be defined in the Unitedstatesian political realist manner that Uribe adopted, which can be summarized as follows. If a state can forcefully dominate the minds and actions of others to be able to realize its goals, then the state has more effective power in relation to those it is competing against for resources, security, and authority to achieve what it wants. Machiavelli and Gramsci informed us that without the stronger making concessions to the weaker to win their consent, it is difficult to realize state aims. Without the consent of the governed or those from whom one wishes cooperation, the state will be in a situation of constant fear of revolution, attack, and non-cooperation, especially if they feel they have been treated unjustly. In short, the non-consenting parties will make it difficult for state aims to move forward and solidify. Thus, a security and defense policy primarily driven by force and coercion can be counter-productive since it creates an emotive, impassioned, and, at times, enraged opposition. Machiavelli and Gramsci acknowledged that for a state to rid itself of anarchy and disorder, action would have to be based on taking into consideration the vulnerable and the weak. They saw a necessity for the state to focus on the art of governing individuals and constructing foreign policy to secure permanent consent.[213]

With this in mind, Machiavelli and Gramsci suggested a dual perspective when dealing with political conflicts: a marriage of force and consent; a centaur—the combination of the beast and the humane.[214] Each used appropriately when called for. Hegemony can then be understood as a science of the state where all the activities used to justify its policies, actions, and authority are not only maintained through force and coercion in the background, but, also, and most importantly, via the active consent of those it governs, from whom it seeks cooperation, or seeks to represent.[215] This is the true test of state legitimacy. What Gramsci reinserted to the discussion of hegemony and transformation was an approach that accounted for the will of the weak and vulnerable.[216]

A state, for Gramsci, was a balance and combination between civil society and political society because, in reality, they are the same.[217] All these social entities need to be understood as an interconnected whole. Not doing so limits not only the ability for collective change but also aids in the repression of the masses. Instead, Gramsci advised that to avoid this error, all these separated parts need to be understood together. The state, thus, would no longer be grasped simply as the government or the economy alone, but the state as equal to civil society plus political society.[218]

This whole he defined as a historic bloc. The historic bloc is to be understood as a dialectic between the structure and superstructure;[219] between the political, legal, cultural, and ideological systems and the economic base and modes and

132

forces of production. Without the understanding of the relationship between structure and superstructure, the many forces that are active in shaping our history cannot be analyzed effectively.[220] For transformation to happen, a union of social forces and power relations needs to occur. This involves moving beyond a specific class or group interest and reaching out to other classes and groups to create alliances. With alliances, knowing when to make compromises with different techniques of power and forces—from both the structure and superstructure levels—is an important element for building a base of consent. A historic bloc could then be one that is already dominant or emerging. If emerging, it needs to be stronger than the previous one to be in an effective position to replace it—as Santos's historic bloc is demonstrating to be when contrasted with Uribe's.[221] If a state like Colombia wants to gain hegemony and friendly cooperation with neighbors, it would have to find a technique of power and order where those parties and individuals within its reach can find some kind of compatibility with Colombia's own collective interests.[222] Santos appears to be succeeding where Uribe failed.

An incorrect analysis of the relationship between structure and superstructure and/or a lack of historic bloc may lead to a crisis of hegemony, authority, and legitimacy, as was the case in the Andean diplomatic crisis and security dilemma. In these instances, consent slips away, whereby certain parties try to hold on to power through force and coercion domestically or internationally, as illustrated by Uribe's unilateral policy of coercion against Colombians and neighbors: anyone Uribe deemed a terrorist or terrorist sympathizer. As Gramsci wrote, there is a crisis of authority when "the ruling class has lost its consensus, i.e. is no longer 'leading' but only 'dominant', hegemony coercive force alone." Furthermore, during this crisis of hegemony, Gramsci continued, the ruling party has difficulty exercising its authority and working toward its intended goals—as expressed with the DSDP under Uribe—

because it is prevented by an uncooperative and resentful opposition.[223]

Though Uribe, while he campaigned in 2002 for the presidency, set out to be a Colombian centaur—hard fisted (the beast), big hearted (the humane)—he came out looking more like an Amazon jaguar stalking prey in a viciously calculated and obsessive manner. What was wrong with Uribe's PC and DSDP and how has it improved under Santos domestically and as a foreign affairs strategy? The policy's effectiveness was limited with Uribe because it neglected to exercise the most fundamental elements of the Machiavellian and Gramscian approaches for successful conflict resolution: the democratic aspect (the humane). Though promised, Uribe instead emphasized the most restricting features of conflict resolution: the obsession with achieving goals via force and coercion (the beast), while simultaneously disregarding the concerns of those who did not pose a dominating threat. In turn, the policy's scope was limited for long-term, meaningful, and sustainable peace and security since what Machiavelli and Gramsci advised against materialized in Colombia: peace that arises from force will produce a desire for revenge and violence among those forced to be peaceful. So, when the opportunity arises, these subjects of forced peace may, or have a desire to, stop cooperating, conspire, or revolt against those who have exercised force against them. As a result, the Uribe Andean diplomatic crisis and security dilemma, since March of 2008, grew out of control only to be relaxed and quieted after the current Santos administration enacted the Machiavellian and Gramscian approaches to conflict resolution.

On Behalf of Colombia's War Children

20 September 2010. *Colombia Reports*

When I lived in Bogotá in 2009, authorities killed Pepe the Hippo, which was one the many exotic animals Pablo Escobar had in his personal zoo on his Napoles ranch estate. For a while, it seemed that café and restaurant conversations mouthed Pepe's name at least once in between bites of ajiaco and sips of tinto. I also remember a newspaper image of a woman protester wearing a hippopotamus mask in solidarity with the poor animal. I was saddened by this. The episode in its entirety illustrated to me how desensitized Colombians had potentially become to the loss of human life.

News and public discourse about the hippopotamus, along with outrage by some, was more prevalent than the humanitarian crisis plaguing the country. Victims of the violence have become so common that Colombians, and the world, quite possibly no longer feel as intensely about human death or human life than they may have if the armed conflict had not been a protagonist for lifetimes of succeeding generations.

Colombians need a cold shower to reawaken our senses, re-sensitize our hearts, and redirect our outrage.

It may be counter-intuitive, but I suggest one way to do this may be by taking a trip into Colombia's heart of darkness: that place inside each one of us we do not want to unpack and unravel because what we may discover could be too disturbing. Feelings of shame, guilt, and hatred could commence to frolic freely, painting our realities with hues and shades we hoped remained hidden in the Crayola box.

We may be able to feel more about the loss of Colombian human life—and thus awaken us from our almost apathetic routine regarding this cancer keeping our people from being able to flourish like the colorful flora adorning our landscapes—if we can put names to combat body counts, if we can place faces on the victims, if we can provide flesh to the bones of the dead and the vulnerable. If we can do this, we may begin to feel sympathy and sadness for our conflict's casualties.

Consider the following part a defense of terrorists.

Yes, someone must do it because if I don't, considering the temperature of contemporary public discourse, who will? I speak about the nation's youth, many of whom are identified as terrorists. As a consequence, the government has justified total war.

Various sources, including the government, claim that up to possibly a third of Colombian terrorist groups are made up of minors. Some have not even been alive long enough to have experienced the turn of the century. They make up the FARC and ELN. They embody city gangs. I ask you, are these terrorists?

Visualize your own child, or nephews, or nieces, or young neighbors kicking Postobón cans up the street. These are the faces of a significant number of Colombia's terrorists. In turn, they are also many of the casualties of the country's terror and subsequent war on terror.

When we think of Colombia's terrorists, we conveniently draw up images of Mono Jojoy or Salvatore Mancuso or George Bush or Álvaro Uribe Vélez. It is easy to channel that anger to such individuals depending on one's political sensibilities. But we forget they are not on the front lines dodging bullets and sidestepping landmines. It is our children.

The same goes for those who fight terrorism in Colombia's security forces. These, too, are made up of the country's youth. Though they may not be minors, most of them are teenagers. Further, the reality is that because of Colombia's legal loophole, which allows the wealthy to purchase military cards that exempt their children from so-called "mandatory" service, it is Colombia's most vulnerable youth who end up statistics of death in this war on terror.

Let's turn the page once again and recognize that only in the past 8 years alone, since Uribe first took office, almost 2.5 million Colombians were forcibly displaced internally and another 2 million left the country—hundreds of thousands of these Colombians were minors.

Who is speaking for their little voices? It is difficult to hear them when most of Colombia does not even want to see their faces. Heck, some high political officials have even publicly rejected their existence by labeling them "migrant workers" instead of refugees. But, even if they were simply "migrant workers," we should still feel sympathy, especially because many of them are children.

We provide labels to these green mangoes that, many times, remove and hide their identities. Words like terrorist, like displaced, like disappeared, make it easier for us to go on with our days and just let the faceless armies of Santos and Cano fight it out.

We have to stop turning the other cheek in this respect in order to see the unwrinkled sadness printed on the canvases of the country's youngest generations.

A couple of recent films—*Pequeñas Voces* (*Little Voices*) and *Los Colores de la Montaña* (*The Colors of the Mountain*)—have done well to give a voice and paint a face to this widespread and systematic humanitarian injustice. The films filter Colombia's armed conflict through the eyes of our children. We must listen. We must ask them what they want. We must reconsider a diplomatic solution. We must end this conflict. We must demand it. If not for us, at least for the nation's children. For what is to come.

When we pay a war tax, when we say no to peaceful negotiations, when we receive U.S. military aid, when we recruit more soldiers to fight this incessant war that has desensitized so many, I want you to remember the face of at least one, just one, Colombian child or teenager—not the face of a hippopotamus or Cano or Santos—and meditate on that child's face, and recognize this is the face of Colombia's future, its legacy, our legacy, who we continue to send into the jungle and foothills to die.

These little voices on the mountain, they are my Pepes. And these words you read, they are the wrinkles on the mask I wear in solidarity.

God's Will, or the Will to Power?

28 February 2011, *Colombia Reports*

The so-called intelligence of a group depends in part on the ignorance of its members. When the soil nourishing the roots of our knowledge goes untilled—when our collective wisdom goes undiscussed, uninvestigated, and uncriticized—it may be our intelligence that stands in the way of our own flourishing.

I write these words with the intention of sparking a much-needed public discourse about the potential positive and negative influences and impacts of a belief widely shared in Colombia: God's will.

We can better deal with human rights abuses, crimes against humanity, forced displacement, economic disparities, homophobia, white supremacy, the patriarchy, political exclusion, impunity, corruption, violence against women and children, and so on, if the lens we use to interpret these problems and to create strategies to ameliorate them is more effective and realistic.

It is important to note from the start that I do not hold this belief in God's will to be the primary source of the problems hindering our development and attainment of security, wealth, health, justice, freedom, and fulfillment. It is, however, an important variable creating specific complications that impede our ability to resolve these issues. I propose we dissect and question such a widely accepted mantra (accepted mostly on faith) if we, as a society, really want to move forward.

Let us begin by asking an almost absurd question: Is Colombia a theocratic state?

When some think of states highly connected to or influenced by a religion, images may surface of the Vatican City or Israel or the Islamic Republic of Iran. And, of course, there are states with theocratic associations, like Saudi Arabia. However, though Colombia is not considered a theocratic state and does not share Saudi Arabia's theocratic overtones, almost every action in politics and everyday life in Colombia is essentially buried deep in the belief in God—more specifically a Catholic God—and that God's will.

In practice, regardless of what the country's constitution or its politicians may claim, Colombia, sadly, looks more and more like a state run and ruled by God's will, while hustling politicians and a largely religious citizenry simply play the role of puppets for the puppeteer.

For starters, more than 90% of Colombia is Roman Catholic and fights strongly to keep things that way. You step out of line, you are Othered, you are looked down upon, you are sinful, you are unethical, immoral, soul-less, unworthy, dirty, uncultured, uneducated, savage, hell-bound, etc. Remember the charge against Antanas Mockus during the most recent presidential election campaign that he was an atheist? This was an attack because being an atheist—i.e., not believing in God's will—was one of the worst things one could be. It's no surprise many believe being an atheist is worse than being a pedophile or a murderer.

In the Colombian home and outside its doors, the atmosphere has never been conducive for unearthing the roots of our beliefs.

It is no surprise it is difficult to break from the Colombian pressure to love some imaginary friend (God). Everywhere the pressure looks at you straight in the eye. Ride a bus, for example, and it will be difficult to not find Catholic paraphernalia or prayers plastered as propaganda on some surface.

Though, directly, there is no gun held to our heads to believe X or Y, the dominant culture and its institutions act as social control mechanisms that limit our own ability to finally be able to think for ourselves without being marginalized, guilt-tripped, or scared to toe the line of a theistic religion that even most Colombians do not follow in action. If we evaluate religiosity not on whether a people say they believe but through their daily habits and practices, most Colombians are religious only in their adherence to the party line and the theistic apathy that comes from a belief in God's divine plan for the nation and its people.

This institutionalized social control mechanism—which pushes such an indoctrination of blind faith and acceptance, that Others those who differ in opinions and beliefs, that has ultimately yielded intolerance and stunted the flourishing of analytic and critical thinking—is disheartening, to say the least.

I see this as one of the major roadblocks and hurdles Colombia faces today.

How can a society flourish, be tolerant and accepting of others, develop, and manifest its passions, dreams, and desires, if the very individuals in said society, by and large, either do not, cannot, or are too afraid to question and pursue such curiosities without being stigmatized or told they are going to burn in hell and be eternally tortured if they step out of line? It begins with the indoctrination of the children and continues thereafter.

This leads me to ask the main question that guides this piece: How can a people deal with its problems—like the armed conflict—if a significant portion of both victims and victimizers tightly hold to the blind belief that what they have done or what others have done to them is the will of God?

During research on Colombia's armed conflict, I have been shocked to find this to be a widely held belief: women who have been raped or sexually violated, peasants forcefully removed from their lands, parents whose children have died in the crossfire of bullets and bombs, and paramilitary warlords who have enacted horrendous violence, for example, believe that everything that occurred was part of God's master plan, that it was God's will.

Such a prevalent disposition should be a red flag that calls for further study and reflection.

Colombia is not destined to be in an armed conflict. Half of Colombians are not destined to be poor and a larger majority are not destined to be exploited. A small percentage of citizens are not destined to own most of the country's wealth. Colombians are not destined to be displaced. The poor are not destined to partake in the Colombian armed forces while the rich can simply buy a military card so their children do not have to partake in the country's so-called "mandatory" military conscription program.

It is not God's will for you to be violated, raped, chopped up into pieces and thrown into a river, for you to be buried in a

142

mass grave, have your home or land taken from you, and so on. Not every Colombian accepts and is guided by the "it was God's will" mantra, but enough do to make it troublesome for the sake of justice, conflict resolution, reparations, and peace.

When the victims of the armed conflict believe the crimes committed against them were God's will, that they must have deserved the injustices committed against them, that they were punished by God for something they did previously, then we have a major social problem.

Social change and progressive transformation is difficult if the most vulnerable members of civil society have accepted crimes against humanity as part of God's plan, if the victims themselves see themselves as the victimizers.

Colombians are a people of action. We are known for our entrepreneurship and our willingness to take up arms for things we believe in. However, when it comes to sincerely dissecting one of the major seeds of our country's problems, we are rather inactive. The institutionalized God's-will attitude has created an apathetic citizenry in certain respects. This situation matters, especially when we deal with conflict resolution and issues of rights, justice, and safety. But things do not have to be the way they are and have been.

Colombians need to re-evaluate beliefs, practices, and traditions—our foundational pillars—if, as individuals and as a collective, we are to manifest our potential.

So, is Colombia a theocratic state? No, not by conventional definitions. But is it run by God? You better believe it is; and this rule, in this author's humble opinion, keeps the country on its knees.

Colombians: Can Old Dogs Learn New Tricks?

19 May 2011, *Colombia Reports*

When we discuss Colombian security, we should note we face more than one threat/conflict keeping us from realizing a more peaceful society. Our very social ethics are also at fault. It may be wise to expand horizons by looking beyond our traditional sources for peace and security strategies. We can learn a lot from the Japanese, for example, about community cohesiveness and respect.

In Colombia, violence does not come solely at the hands of armed groups. We speak less about how we ourselves, in our daily interactions, treat each other with little dignity and little respect for the concerns of others. From the way we drive to how we try to hustle potential customers when conducting business, we seem to act solely with our singular selves in mind.

When individuals are treated *merely* as means to an end, their dignity as humans is said to be violated. We become understood simply as commodities, as properties, as objects, as things that can be exploited, exchanged, and/or eliminated for the sake of selfish ends. It is with this definition of violence I proceed and where most of the Japanese differ from most Colombians.

Our cultural disposition toward fellow neighbors is rooted in serving the self over, or at the expense of, the community. When the concerns of others are not considered, such disrespect becomes fertile ground for aggression, hostility, and exploitation. In turn, trust in one's fellow human is very seldom given, which makes it difficult to foster a secure, organized, ordered, and peaceful community.

Sadly, the conventional Colombian ethic suggests that if you do not take advantage of others when they are weak or vulnerable, then you are a fool. Common expressions like "no de papaya" (don't draw attention to yourself) illustrate the notion that individuals are constantly looking for targets to exploit and you should prepare yourself for potential exploitation.

Recently, Kenji Orito Díaz received a Humanitarian and Volunteer Service honor. During his speech, though unintended, an example he gave underscores our impudent culture. Orito Díaz spoke of how truly rich Colombians are because in Japan it can cost 160,000 pesos for a watermelon they may only have access to in August. He contrasted this with the fact that in Colombia, where such a treat is abundant, even when the fruit seller charges only 5,000 pesos for the melon, "one is so [shameless] that one tells the gentleman 'I only have 3,000'."

The word Orito Díaz used was "descarado," which literally means "faceless." While in Colombia this type of "faceless" act is common, in Japan the complete opposite is the case: saving face, not losing it, is the social ethic. The watermelon example was glossed over as a joke by speaker and audience because

145

this behavior is so widespread, thereby highlighting our habitual tendency to disregard the needs and concerns of others.

In the narrative bubble where most Colombians reside, there exists the belief that how humans behave in Colombia is how all humans behave everywhere. But such is, of course, not the case.

Living in Japan for the better part of 2010, I was shocked many times into realizing how different social ethics are between the Japanese and Colombians.

The way the Japanese have dealt with their recent crises via water (tsunami), earth (quake), and air (nuclear radiation) is testimony to the influence of their belief systems, institutions, and social ethics. If such disasters had occurred in Colombia, it would not surprise many if riots and disturbances would have transpired. Yet, though Japan was slammed with the first recorded triple disaster in history, no riots or social disruptions arose. On this basis alone, the Japanese deserve our attention. They have been doing something right. They proved that such social cohesion, respect, and community is possible, not a fantasy, and, conversely, disproved the idea that such a society (even one of 127 million people) could never exist.

Such an attitude, however, is not only enacted during crisis, but also in everyday life.

A Colombian traveling through Japan may think the Japanese are fools for being too trusting. Yet, the kind of exploitation and violations of another's dignity is seldom found in Japan, but habitually found in Colombia.

True story: A woman parked her car, left it running with a baby in the back seat, and walked into the grocery store. Fifteen minutes passed before she returned to car and baby with two bags of groceries by her side. I observed the entire incident from my bicycle. I waited until the woman returned because I feared a potential car theft or a kidnapping. The Japanese community would have been shocked if the car *was* stolen or if the baby *was* kidnapped. The Colombian community, on the other hand, would have been shocked if the car *wasn't* stolen and the baby *wasn't* kidnapped.

I can leave my wallet on the table with USD $300 worth of yen visibly sticking out, leave the cafe for 20 minutes to talk on my mobile, then return to find my wallet untouched. A businessman who has missed his train and must sleep in the station overnight does not have to worry that his briefcase will be stolen while he sleeps.

The Japanese have demonstrated that equipping a police force with firearms is not a necessary and sufficient condition for a society to be relatively peaceful, secure, organized, ordered, and civil. Compare that with Colombians' historical obsession with primarily using arms to achieve peace.

Criminologist and father of Social Control Theory Travis Hirschi may have been on to something when he wrote the following:

> We are all animals and thus all naturally capable of committing criminal acts. [...] People commit crimes because it is in their nature to do so. The question that really needs an answer is why do most people *not* commit crimes?

"Delinquency," Hirschi claimed, "is not caused by beliefs that require delinquency, but rather made possible by the absence of (effective) beliefs that forbid delinquency." Colombians' belief system not only requires delinquency to understand reality, human nature, and the world and one's place in it, but also lacks effective beliefs that forbid delinquency. Japan's beliefs, on the other hand, are there to ensure people are secured from delinquent and hostile acts.

There's a lot we can learn from the Japanese that deserves careful study, which this is not. However, it should be a start to challenge and dissect our presuppositions because Japan completely resides outside the box of the reality most Colombians have pronounced as absolute and universal. This should be the first step in potentially changing a belief system—recognizing it is unsound and limited. Just as we have looked at the Bible and the U.S. for ways to deal with our security issues, we should potentially look at other regions and societies of the world to see what may be applicable to our situation.

There are many interpretations of human nature and reality, and some have proven more effective for satisfying human concerns. For example, we must get past the Colombian idea that morality can only be derived from the dictates of the Bible. Belief in a god is not a necessary and sufficient condition for living ethically and for treating others with kindness. In many ways, Catholicism's influence in the country has been a hindrance. It has led to the rejection of other interpretations of reality and human nature that could help to manifest a more peaceful society. It is time to look abroad to other codes of ethics for guidance.

We do not have to wait for government action for the quality of our lives to be heightened even a little and for our daily interactions to be more enjoyable. We can help the matter by changing our habits and choosing to conduct ourselves differently. As Gandhi so eloquently claimed, what distinguishes human animals "from all other animals" is our "capacity to be non-violent." The Japanese have come to understand this idea quite well. It is an integral part of their cultural attitude toward conflict resolution and community building. What is remarkable is that their history, for centuries, was steeped and tainted with violence, until the middle of the 20th century.

So, can Colombians learn anything from the Japanese in terms of social ethics? Contrary to popular belief, in the dog-eat-dog world where most Colombians believe they reside, there may be a possibility for teaching old dogs new, more respectful, tricks.

Save the Water for a Rainy Colombian Day

31 May 2011, *Colombia Reports*

In a time when Colombians are sick and tired of water because of the incessant torrential rains that have hit the country since last year, in a time during Colombia's worst natural disaster in its history that has affected more than 3 million people and flooded over 2.5 million acres of land, in a time when we have welcomed with open arms President Juan Manuel Santos's declaration this week that the weather phenomenon of La Niña is finally over, I am here to tell you we should not shelve our water concerns just yet.

I predict one of the most pressing issues of this century for Colombia is learning to cope with the growing needs of water and sanitation within cities.

Let's contextualize the issue.

Because of its salt content, 97.5% of earth's water is not suitable for drinking (UN Human Development Report). This leaves 2.5% of freshwater for our consumption. However, less than 1% of the freshwater is readily accessible to us, with about 70% of it stored in ice caps. Colombia is one of six countries (along with Brazil, Canada, China, Indonesia, and Russia) that houses 50% of the world's freshwater reserves. You would think with so much freshwater Colombia would be one of the few countries that would not have water concerns, but it should.

Though Colombia is one of the six countries that hosts much of the world's freshwater, that freshwater is threatened with contamination and drying up. For example, half of the country's departments have registered contaminated drinking water. More appalling is that only 12.5% of departments offer water safe for consumption. The situation has left 15% of departments to offer "high risk" water to their residents.

Colombia's potable water shortage is cause for panic, and the reasons should alarm you because the factors are increasingly negatively affecting our water problem. With the impact of global warming and as we move forward with industrialization projects, we have traded our water, forests, and agricultural land for a greater GDP. A few major environmental issues are rooted in extensive deforestation and soil and water damage correlated to the overuse of pesticides, for example. This has helped make Colombia a high-risk destination for major infectious diseases. Food and waterborne diseases, like bacterial diarrhea, and water contact diseases, like leptospirosis, will continue to remain high risk diseases, or get worse, if we do not address the water issue as a major threat to our security.

Further, as freshwater becomes more scarce and polluted, it will become a highly sought resource with the potential to spark wars, like oil has in the 20th and 21st centuries. Countries with the power to do so will do what they can to get their hands on such freshwater reserves either by means of cooperation, soft power, or hard power. Since Colombia is one of the top-six water reserves in the world, the country is bound to become of great interest, like the oil producing countries have been during our oil age.

Another factor to keep in mind is that Colombia's population is becoming more and more urbanized. With 75% of Colombians living in urban areas (2010) and with an annual urbanization rate of change of 1.7% (estimates for 2010-2015), we must anticipate potential future water concerns. The fact that 45.5% (2009) of Colombians live below the poverty line and that distribution of family income is getting worse—Gini index: 53.8 (1996), 58.5 (2009); Colombia now the 8th worst in the world for income inequality—we can anticipate near and long-term threats affecting a large percentage of our population.

Many Colombians live in slums or informal settlements that are scattered around the country's cities. One main challenge that will continue to evolve is providing our poor with adequate water and sanitation facilities. According to the UN's Water and Cities Facts and Figures, around the world "the urban poor pay up to 50 times more for a liter of water than their rich neighbors, since they often have to buy their water from private vendors." Colombia has not been immune to this international phenomenon.

In April and May of this year, for example, large parts of Medellín went without running water for weeks after landslides destroyed part of the city's water supply network. As a resident impacted by the water shortage claimed, "They are selling water, but I have not seen one water truck here." During this water shortage, Medellín residents complained that the available water the EPM (Medellín's public services enterprises) finally delivered was not clean, which resulted in giving residents stomach problems, diarrhea, and cause for vomiting. In 2008, Colombians with the country's lowest 10% household income consumed only 0.8% of the country's share of goods, while the highest 10% consumed 45%. With the economic disparity being as large as it is, we can anticipate a potential future threat regarding adequate water for a large portion of the country's poor and vulnerable population.

Along with a desire for democracy and more jobs, many of the political changes going on in the Arab world now also concern the current rise in food prices. We should not think lightly of the issue. Food prices are also rising in Colombia, and the water situation is getting worse. Water is a major security issue and should be a variable in the country's policy of Democratic Security and Defense. The government, however, has been quite pathetic when dealing with this topic by not having a clear strategy for managing land and controlling water sources. This needs to change.

The government, however, is not entirely at fault nor are we utterly helpless. For one thing, we can be more careful and cautious about the amount of water we use as individuals and allow companies to waste. Because of the constant rains caused by La Niña, Colombians may never have seen this much water. Yet, as our lands become inundated, we are on a slow path toward water shortage, a water crisis. The more we let water flow through our faucets when it is not needed, the closer we are to a thirsty future for all.

Colombians speak of the "sin" it is to waste food. "¡Qué pecado!" says my grandmother. Yet, for some reason, we do not think of water as food when we go about our day: taking showers, brushing teeth, washing dishes, mopping floors, washing cars, watering lawns (often simply for aesthetic value), consuming products that require an enormous amount of water to produce and transport, and so on. Despite this, without water there is no food. Without water there is no life. Period.

Further, along with not treating water as a food, we treat it as if it were an infinite resource. This waste of water may be partly rooted in the interpretation of a very contentious verse in the Bible—the so-called Dominion Mandate in Genesis 1:28—where it states the following:

> And God blessed them [Adam and Eve], and God said unto them, be fruitful, and multiply, and replenish the Earth, and *subdue* it: and have *dominion* over the fish of the sea, and over the fowl of the air, and over every living thing that moveth upon the Earth. (Italics mine.)

In short, there's a widespread belief that "God" has made the world and everything in it for humans, and, thus, we can do whatever we want with the resources without consequence.

The waste may also be rooted in the ignorance about how our lifestyle and everyday consumption patterns use water. For example, according to The Conservation Blog of The Nature Conservancy, there are many things we could do to save water if we simply learned the facts about hidden water and how to conserve more. Below are some examples The Nature Conservancy provides:

- It takes 1,800 gallons of water to grow enough cotton to make a pair of jeans.
- It takes 2,192 gallons of water to make 1 pound of leather.
- Use a rain barrel to water your petunias. They can store 50-80 gallons of water.
- A garden hose can use 530 gallons of water/hour.
- The water footprint of a pound of beef is 1,500 gallons.
- You can lose 20 gallons of water per day from one drippy faucet.
- Cut your shower time by 5 minutes and save up to 20 gallons of water per shower.
- Turn off the water while brushing and shaving and save up to 1,000 gallons/month.

- It takes 24 gallons of water to make a pound of plastic.
- Eat healthily: It takes 49 gallons of water to make a bag of chips, but 18 to grow an apple.

Forecasting the future is always an uncertain business, but I am sure of the following two things: (1) We must demand from our government a clear plan of action to manage land, regulate companies' water usage, and control water sources, and (2) we need to be more cautious as individuals about how we use/waste water. If we don't, the 21st century may provide the stage for an inundated world that slowly dies of thirst.

Contextualizing Colombian Development Amidst the Armed Conflict: Fear and Hope for Canada's Role in the Extractive Industry

April 2013

In Latin America, we learn early that our lives are worth little.

Laura Yusem[224]

In the struggle for land, human life in Colombia has been devalued.

Herbert Braun[225]

There's a huge exploration boom in gold, and it's being led by foreigners, and it's being led by Canadian companies.

Mauricio Cardenas, Colombian Mines and Energy Minister[226]

Introduction

As Colombia and Canada look toward development, what can both governments and Canadian multinational corporations (MNCs) in the extractive sector do to not exacerbate the armed conflict? The veins of Latin America have been reopened, and Colombia is no exception. Unlike the era of conquest, however, this time the pillaging comes by invitation under the guise of development. Nevertheless, I argue that despite consensual agreements between the Colombian state and other governments and MNCs, for sustainable development and lasting security to transpire in Colombia we need to consider a more holistic, transformative methodology and attitude. Since current policies pushed by MNCs and both Canadian and Colombian governments resemble those that originally gave rise to the armed conflict more than half a century ago, we must be careful to not commit similar mistakes. Without a comprehensive, context-specific approach to conceptualizing development during armed conflict, Colombia will remain under the tutelage of violence, which will continue to wax and wane for time indefinite.

Since much of the current violence is predicated on differing views about how we should organize Colombia to maximize potential and power, we should apply a critical approach to contemporary presumptions about progress. A top-down model that predominantly focuses on force and coercion to achieve goals and disregards the concerns and grievances of the people, especially the most vulnerable populations—such as Afro-descendants, Amerindians, peasants, women, children, the displaced, and other victims of the armed conflict—is short-sighted and counter-productive. Such a model creates an atmosphere of resentment that breeds a strong desire for revenge and noncooperation. We should more carefully take into consideration the positives and negatives of previous development projects enacted in Colombia and the reputation of Canadian corporations before we introduce new policies. Is

Canada's recent role in Colombia via the mining and energy sectors a positive one for the South American country?

Considering Colombia is currently confronted with many opportunities and limitations as it moves toward fulfilling development objectives, we should also address the following related questions: How can resource extraction facilitate development in a war-torn country like Colombia? What can MNCs and Colombian and Canadian governments do to fulfil ambitions and calm historical fires of resentment toward Western-styled development projects? What can be done to thwart potential counter-movements that may give rise to noncooperation and armed resistance? Can civil society grievances be adequately addressed during this new renaissance of subsoil resource exploration and exploitation?

Present policies must make room for a diverse discourse regarding how to more effectively use our resources—natural and human—to benefit Colombia's project of regeneration and transformation. For such goals to be effectively managed, social and environmental ills must be intelligently and sincerely considered. Profit must not be the only conductor on the locomotive toward progress in Colombia. Previous implemented notions of development—specifically after 1949 when President Harry S. Truman introduced the U.S.'s first plan for international economic development—exacerbated existing internal conflicts and have demonstrated to be unsustainable. If our predominant concern is with obstacles keeping the country from realizing its full potential, we cannot sacrifice the environment, human rights, and our moral compass for the sake of the capital instant gratification of a few. Economic growth is merely a tool—a means to realize other ends. If what we deem most valuable and sacred are sacrificed for the sake of the means, we welcome a cure worse than the disease. If policies are short-sighted, so too will be rewards. So too will be progress and security.

Is Canada's presence a cure worse than the disease? Twenty-first-century Colombia faces a dilemma as it tries to balance sustainable development and economic growth, while simultaneously engaged in the world's longest-running domestic armed conflict. With such a concern at hand, we must cast a wider net. I forward the following four obstacles as potential answers to why after World War Two the U.S. model of development aggravated already existing conflicts in Colombia, and why, if left unchecked, such an approach will continue to be a significant obstacle in the country's quest to manifest its full potential, especially as the mining and energy sectors continue to rapidly grow: historical lack of hegemony and institutionalized violence; unstable and unsustainable development practices; irresponsible and unaccountable corporate relationships; and a disregard for human rights and the environment.

Let's dissect the various components of failed progress in Colombia to better interpret development amidst the backdrop of the armed conflict.

Historical lack of hegemony and institutionalized violence

Manuel Rozental[227] was correct to paint Colombia's history with the following pattern: people are massacred or enslaved, displaced, the land is freed, and the élite, foreign powers, and multi-national corporations come in to exploit the land and the labor force.[228] It was not until the middle of the 20th century that this pattern was followed by a significant counter-movement, which gave rise to the armed conflict in its present form. It has been these power struggles that have led Colombia to what it is today—a continuous constellation of weak and frail societies-in-transition. Since Colombia is by no means a mature nation-state, we must take care to not implement a-historical, context-less, one-size-fits-all development and security models. If the complex domestic dimensions of Colombia's state-building are neglected, especially its security predicament, the pattern Rozental described may not be broken.

Power is conventionally defined as the ability to influence or impose either an individual's or a collective's will onto others. Politics, in turn, becomes the struggle and competition for public power and authority that will give a person or a group the ability to make decisions for or to implement the desires of the larger group, or both. Traditionally, political science textbooks offer two avenues of political organization—consensus (democratic rule) and coercion (authoritarian rule). When the former path is taken, individuals tend to band together for the sake of protection and to create common rules. Civil society chooses leadership from among the people, and security is achieved by cooperation. When the latter path is taken, individuals are brought together by a ruler who imposes authority and monopolizes power. Security, on this path, comes through domination.

As far as these either/or textbook definitions go, we cannot easily fit Colombia into either camp, as it is neither a mature democracy nor a dictatorship. Colombia falls on a spectrum not only between the two paths of political organization noted above but has also experienced both situations at the same time to different degrees. Nazih Richani was correct to point out that despite significant changes during these past two centuries, the country "has never moved beyond a fragmented sovereignty" because it continues to be shared with regional caudillos, paramilitary organizations, guerrilla groups, traditional élites, and the contemporary narco-bourgeoisie.[229] In addition, as Miguel Eduardo Cárdenas Rivera and Felipe Díaz Chávez wrote, we can also attribute such sovereign fragmentation to the country's submissive experience with the international bourgeoisie, transnational corporations, and global powers.[230] Marco Palacios, in his work *Between Legitimacy and Violence: A History of Colombia, 1875-2002*, identified this ineffective marriage between consent and coercion well when he stated that Colombia "is a permanent framework of legitimacy and violence, and even though its institutions are facades, they provide resources and the rules of the game to everyone, even the guerrillas."[231]

When we construct conflict resolution and development strategies, it would be wise to adopt an interpretive lens that can effectively explain and describe the past and predict the future. If this lens is inadequate, so too will plans of action we devise to manifest desired objectives. In the case of Colombia, Mohammed Ayoob's insights can lead us to better understand its history: "The more primitive the stage of state-making and the more incomplete the state's capacity to control and/or gain the acquiescence of the large majority of its population, the greater the possibility of internal conflict and disorder."[232] Add to this scenario the facts that Colombia has one of the most difficult terrains[233] in Latin America, is a country whose distribution of wealth is one of the world's worst, continues to experience violent and non-violent oppression at the hands of the government and illegally armed groups, has incessantly suffered from political exclusion, and endures a species of economic greed run rampant, and the goal of unity and development becomes extremely complicated. It is precisely this situation that has overwhelmed the country. Two centuries since Simón Bolívar spoke his words and drew his sword in the name of liberation and self-determination, Colombia's conflict not only lingers but endures.

Since Colombia's birth in the early 1800s, the following have not existed as parts of a whole, let alone as a total package:

- an effective state able to establish sovereignty,
- a monopoly of force by the state,
- a state able to effectively develop and distribute public goods and property rights,
- a state able to resist corruption, and
- entities that have allowed for the transfer of power between governments of the time.

Though Colombia's capacity to attend to these hindrances has waxed and waned throughout the years, it has continuously been either unsuccessful or weak in all abovementioned arenas. Unless we effectively deal with these issues, it will be difficult to claim with any certainty that Colombia's long history of violence will cease to exist any time soon.

Power-sharing is not something for which Colombia is known. This situation is largely due to several reasons: a mistrust that elected representatives will act in either the interest of the traditional system, corporations, narco-bourgeoisie, and/or global powers instead of the people's; the difficulty posed by the terrain to unify the country; and epistemological reasons— such as a pre-modern, feudal understanding of the world and how power, hegemony, and development should be achieved. Further, because of the fragmented sovereignty delineated above, inadequate power-sharing mechanisms have made the environment difficult for citizens and other groups to regard the government as legitimate. Considering these obstacles, different entities with the capacity to enact soft and hard power and impose authority have not, for the most part, allowed for the smooth transfer of power between governments.

Within this fragmented sovereignty, Colombia has continually and simultaneously walked both paths of political organization. It is concurrently democratic and authoritarian, consensual and coercive. Historically, violence in Colombia has been understood as the most flagrant manifestation of power. This relationship has been a hindrance to establishing lasting security and a strong, effective, and legitimate modern nation-state. Violence has been recognized as both means *and* end. The result of this understanding of power has only led to violence becoming institutionalized; thereby making it difficult for more legitimate and cooperative mechanisms to flourish.

This pattern needs to be broken if the goal is any semblance of sustainable development and lasting peace and security. No

162

matter how much money people, organizations, and countries throw at aid, development, and security programs; no matter if the government returns land to displaced persons; no matter if we put laws in place to repair and protect victims of crimes, none of these efforts will make significant dents in resolving the armed conflict and allowing Colombia to realize its potential if the state

- cannot effectively implement policy;
- is not trust-worthy, transparent, and legitimate;
- cannot produce results in fair and just ways; and
- cannot, *simultaneously*, secure the public.

Unfortunately, since state institutions are also responsible for some of the worst violations of human rights in the country—over 3,000 extrajudicial executions between 2002 and 2010, for instance—the state is also feared. As a result, anything we do to supposedly better the lives and situations of Colombians will have minimal, short-term impact and will act only as a temporary bandage.

Perpetual state infrastructural weakness has been at the root of Colombia's historical lack of hegemony and its institutionalized bellicose culture. In conjunction with the usual explanations, it is the fragmented nation-state—feudal and fractured by its demanding terrain—that has set the parameters for the power struggle that has shaped the country's armed conflict. As Alex McDougall pointed out, "the absence of a strong state presence, combined with the availability of lootable resources explains and predicts the patterns of rebel consolidation in Colombia." It is precisely these "patterns of historical state weakness" that help explain "how Colombia's three major armed groups have formed, developed, and mounted continual challenges to the sovereignty and territorial integrity of the Colombian state."[234]

In short, the powers that be have historically treated Colombian lives with little importance. Instead, they have dealt with Colombians as if they were mere instruments, commodities, and expendable objects used to maximize the power and wealth of a select few. The state and other major actors, by their direct and indirect support of using force and coercion to achieve self-interests, continue to increase the probability of internal conflict and disorder. The pattern persists and could be intensified with the current boom in the mining and energy sectors if this new era is not managed with greater dedication to respecting human rights, the environment, and consensual cooperation.

The struggle for power: movement/countermovement

Colombia's lack of hegemony and institutionalized violence hit a critical point in April of 1948 with El Bogotázo and the start of La Violencia. What germinated set the stage for a movement/countermovement regarding notions of development—a struggle that continues to this day. As Robert Cox observed, most world violence has occurred because of a forceful claim of a universal truth.[235] The one truth disposition—that not only exists, but also can be discovered and applied—has been the foundation for many justifications of forcing others to subvert.[236] The Other—a victim of white supremacy, misogyny, free trade, or collateral damage from a violent guerrilla movement trying to manifest a communist economic model, for instance—is then reified and treated as an object.[237] Amidst the backdrop of trying to control social structures, the West, Colombian institutions, MNCs, neo-paramilitaries, and guerrillas, for example, have created these identities to gain power and authority over individuals and to justify authoritarian practices and violent resistance.

Colombia is still an immature society-in-transition where different notions of development are at odds. The violent struggle for control over how to order and organize the

country continues. It is with this in mind that the FARC
Secretariat released the following statement on 26 March 2013
during peace talks with the Colombian government: "It is
unrealistic to pretend that the conversations between the
government and the insurgency, to put an end to the conflict
and set the bases for a stable peace, do not touch upon the
economic model."[238] Since the times of La Violencia and the
U.S.'s first plan for international economic investment in 1949,
much of the armed conflict in Colombia has been focused on
disagreements regarding how to better organize Colombia to
realize its maximum potential. During the Cold War, the
development discourse was led by the two super powers of the
time and their respective economic models—the U.S. and
capitalism and the U.S.S.R. and communism.

The U.S. emerged from World War Two as a superpower
whose understanding of and attitude toward the international
community has predominantly been political realist and
economic neo-liberal in nature. With this newfound power,
imperialistic tendencies to change the world order to benefit
U.S. interests became dominant. Economic and political
freedoms as understood through liberalism and competitive
capitalism have been its world reconstruction goal, of which
Colombia was a part. The U.S. deems its capitalist version of
freedom as a universal truth, birthright, and a non-negotiable
demand of every human. It is such ideas—and U.S. and
Colombian action to fulfill them—that have drawn
controversy and retaliation in Colombia.

Post-WWII, Western interests, led by the U.S., proposed that
only in a truly free and private, competitive capitalistic market
would individuals' potential be realized, and freedom not be
infringed. In turn, to guarantee development, a certain
relationship between economics and politics was needed.[239]
Too much political control over commerce, trade, and
transactions would infringe upon individual freedom. The role
of government should be limited to "determining the 'rules of
the game,'"[240] to act "as an umpire to interpret and enforce the

rules decided on,"[241] and to prevent an individual from interfering with another's activities. Decentralizing, limiting, and redirecting the power of government on the individual while applying a free private enterprise exchange competitive economy would allow for and uphold individual liberty and would create the conditions for humans to achieve their full potentials. "[E]conomic freedom [...] promotes political freedom," Milton Friedman argued, "because it separates economic power from political power and in this way enables the one to offset the other."[242] By removing restrictions of economic controls and giving the masses suffrage and the ability to participate in the market would make it so the masses "would do what is good for them." Here, the free-marketeers claim, full political and economic freedom is achieved because the coercion of a person over another is removed.[243] In such an environment, all parties transacting benefit from the transaction.[244] They forwarded that without such economic and political freedoms that create a voluntary cooperative state between people, the typical state of mankind is tyranny, servitude, and misery.

The above is essentially what Francis Fukuyama justified when he stated, "we have reached a point of history where ideological evolution has stopped, for we have reached the ultimate universal truth as how to organize and co-ordinate our world: economic and political liberalism."[245] Historical progression had led toward a secular, free-market democracy, and the end of the Cold War was the ultimate sign that humanity's ideological evolution had reached its conclusion.[246] Fukuyama argued that the final universal truth becomes manifest in the material world, creating the material world in its own image.[247] Fukuyama took on a triumphalist attitude and belief that his particular ideology was superior to all others, and justified it in terms of history having decided so.[248]

The U.S. has based its foreign policies on the above interpretation of history and has used it to justify its quest to reconstruct the world in the image of liberal, competitive capitalism. Until competitive capitalism is universally practiced, the U.S. has seen it reasonable to use its political, economic, propaganda, and military institutions to aid in making the whole world into this image.[249] The free-marketeers recognize free trade as the most comprehensive strategy to manifest real human freedom[250] and the U.S. denounced any governments with a heavy hand and control over their own economies.[251] Therefore, the U.S. has viewed the economy as a direct threat to its liberty and self-interests on the same level as political and military threats.[252]

Since the mid-1960s, wanting to contain full-scale economic liberalism's growth in Colombia, the current two main guerrilla groups—FARC (Marxist-Leninist) and ELN (Marxism combined with liberation theology)—have fought to replace a capitalist Colombian government with a government-led Marxian type of communism. The main concern for these groups, as well as others critical of the Western-Northern style of development, has been that economics ceased to be a tool to help ameliorate human lives, and rather became an end whereby humanity became of secondary importance to profit. There was/is a fear in many sectors of society—though not all in line with the guerrillas' methods—that such a system would ultimately disregard the concerns of most people it was supposed to be taking care. In Colombia, for example, Karl Polanyi's critique of laissez-faire capitalism—that the idea of a self-regulating market with natural and self-healing virtues could never work, has never existed, and is a myth because it is a public organization that is regularly being intervened upon by the government and other institutions—is very much alive and armed.[253]

In Colombia, this intervention is exemplified using force and coercion to manifest it, the funding by the U.S. and other sources to sustain the force, and the laws enacted to create and maintain it. One of the major concerns of free-market liberalism is that it subordinates human purposes to the logic of an impersonal market mechanism. In this process, rapid transformation—as we have seen in Colombia more rigorously since it officially applied neoliberal economic policies in 1990—occurs without ever first putting in place new coping mechanisms and the proper infrastructure to deal with the change. In this sense, the guerrillas have believed that the market should not be thought of as some entity separate from political society and civil society, but as part of a broader economy that was part of a broader society. In this manner, it is the economy that should be subordinated to individual and collective needs, to fundamental ends and human purposes, instead of the other way around.

The guerrillas and other critics of the capitalist model of development have seen it as benefiting the Colombian and foreign bourgeoisie instead of the clear majority of Colombians. The fact that Colombia is one of the most unequal countries in the world when it comes to income and wealth disparity—Gini index wavering between 51.32 and 60.68 since 1980—while the country's GDP has multiplied five-fold since the turn of the century has not made a strong case for trickle-down economics in Colombia. David Harvey's declaration that "Neoliberalism confers rights and freedoms on those whose incomes, leisure, and security need no enhancing; leaving a pittance for the rest of us"[254] rings true to those opposing laissez-faire economics in Colombia. In trying to create a free market system, labor, land, and money were turned into commodities, which ultimately yielded the resistance that continues today. Society became the accessory of the economic system.[255] These changes, critics of neoliberalism claim, continue to destroy all other traditional forms of basic social order that have existed for many cultures—especially in the peasant, artisanal, Afro-Colombian, and Amerindian communities. It is worth pointing out that though the U.S. expects the world to adopt economic liberalism overnight, the U.S. has never done so itself.[256]

Polanyi's claim that resistance is a natural response when a mechanism—in this case the manifestation of a laissez-faire market economy—tries to separate itself and people from the fabric of society is very much the case in the Colombian context.[257] Critics assert that such a system is unsustainable and unstable since it is destructive to basic human concerns—such as, our relationships to ourselves, others, land, labor, and life activity. As a response to the alienating effects of laissez-faire capitalism, spontaneous opposition occurs because society's old safety nets used for order and survival have been eliminated or suppressed. Considering this, the insurgency has deemed itself the army of the people and claim to protect them from the unrestrained free market. In Colombia, the Cold War never ended, and it has always been a hot war. The struggle continues, and these two very polar, top-down views regarding development—the free market vs. a people/state-controlled economy—have stretched well into the 21st century.

The reopened veins of Colombia

The Colombia government is promoting the corporate and foreign take-over of Colombia in neo-colonial fashion. The present is reminiscent of the region's colonial past, as government institutions have also been largely responsible for what Manuel Rozental described as the current of patterns underscoring Colombia's history. The country is rapidly increasing its dependence on the export of non-renewable resources, while simultaneously sacrificing renewable resources. This dependency is constituted by what Asad Ismi deemed "the virtual give-away of precious national resources to foreign companies."[258] Furthermore, like the times of Spanish conquest, not only is environmental degradation taking place, but humans are also being sacrificed for the sake of valuable subsoil resources and their profits. The violent and exploitative pattern persists and could be intensified if the major players do not dedicate themselves to respecting human rights, the environment, and consensual cooperation.

As stated above, Colombia's history is marked with an affront to human dignity by treating the masses as merely a means to an end. The objective for the forcible displacement of persons in Colombia, for example, has largely been politically and economically motivated. Millions of hectares have been appropriated illegally, mostly by the government and government-allied paramilitaries, to use the land, exploit its resources, and enter the products into the global market.[259] Since Consultancy for Human Rights and Displacement (CODHES) started monitoring displaced persons in 1985, over five million have been registered, making Colombia the worst place in the world for internal refugees. By 2010, the cultivation of African palm oil, for instance, had made Colombia the second largest producer of the product in the world. However, Jorge Rojas, director of CODHES, claimed there was a direct correlation between the industry and displacement: "In almost every case where there is a big palm-oil development, there is widespread forced displacement."[260] Such monitoring organizations have also made similar correlations in the energy and mining sectors.

Until recently, the country's history of violence and lacking hegemony created an insecure investment climate. Such an environment kept many governments and MNCs, especially those in the mining and energy sectors, away from Colombia's vastly unexplored and untapped regions. Spending millions of dollars on projects was a dangerous risk not worth taking for most because the Colombian government could not effectively provide security. The fact Colombia was teetering on failed-state status at the turn of the century further fueled fears. The country was vulnerable and so was investor confidence.

However, from 2002 onwards, investors began to gain assurance by way of new economic and security policies enacted under the administrations of Álvaro Uribe Vélez (7 August 2002 - 7 August 2010) and Juan Manuel Santos (7 August 2010 - present). Uribe's platform was prioritized as follows: (1) Establish a monopoly of violence throughout the entirety of Colombia to (2) secure capital investment. Only thereafter would (3) social welfare concerns be confronted.

The following was outlined by the Ministry of Defense annual report as Uribe's "Virtuous Circle": security investment ➔ confidence and stability ➔ private investment ➔ economic growth ➔ social investment ➔ social welfare ➔ security investment ➔ and so on in the cycle.[261] In short, only by the government defeating illegally armed groups and attracting capital investment could it properly engage the welfare of the people.

Santos, Minister of National Defense (19 July 2006 - 18 May 2009) during Uribe's second term, played a leading role in using the country's armed forces to manifest Uribe's "Virtuous Circle." The security and capital investment gains between 2002 and 2010 allowed the current Santos administration to identify mining and energy development as a strategically crucial economic engine thereafter—the "economic locomotive" that is driving and will continue to steer the country's economic growth, according to the president. As reported by Colombia's Central Bank, from 1999 to 2012 Foreign Direct Investment (FDI) grew from US$1.508b to almost US$16b—more than 80 percent concentrated in the oil and mining sectors. Mining sector investment grew from US$464m to US$2,546m while investment in the oil sector increased ten-fold from US$511m to US$5,083m. According to the World Bank, GDP production has been steadily rising from US$80.2602m in 1999 to US$304.5241m in 2011. GDP per capita also steadily grew from US$2,204.1 to US$7,104.03 during the same time span. The Uribe-Santos era can be remembered for its Democratic Security and Defense Policy as well as for its pro-business stance because of the two leaders' ambitious collaborations with the private sector.

Given the country's improved security climate, economic prospects grew; thereby propelling Colombia's standing both regionally and globally. The Fraser Institute identified Colombia as the third most attractive destination for investment in Latin America and one of the world's most desirable for mining. According to the World Bank, despite the internal armed conflict, Colombia has become the most secure country in Latin America to do business. This scenario is mostly due to the Colombian government allocating tens of thousands of armed forces personnel to protect the assets and interests of MNCs. Further, with an economy that has grown four times faster than Canada's in the past decade and FDI numbers that quadrupled between 2002 and 2008 alone, Colombia now boasts a GDP of over USD$400 billion—the fourth largest economy in Latin America. Colombia now has the fastest gas and oil production growth in the world. During Uribe's reign, mining claims in the country ballooned from 2.8 million acres to 21 million. By 2012, it was estimated that 40 percent of the country was under consideration for mining projects. Scotiabank's CEO Rick Waugh believed such trends are only going to grow, which is why the bank has recently partnered with major Colombian institutions to provide capital for Colombian mining and energy companies to help ramp up exploration and production.

The roles of Canada's corporations in the mining and energy sectors have been significant in this process and will continue to be a major player. Over 60 percent of the globe's publicly traded mining companies are listed in the Toronto stock exchange. Canadian MNCs have invested over $40 billion in Latin America, including over 1,000 mining properties. Colombia has attracted many of these companies during the past decade. Through 2010, Canadian MNCs had already invested $824 million in Colombia. The above estimate that 40 percent of Colombia was under consideration for mining projects by 2012 was largely due to what some are calling the "Canadian invasion." The Colombia-Canada Free Trade Agreement (CCFTA), which went into effect August of 2011, has only helped move the Santos economic train forward. The Canadian government, led by Prime Minister Stephen Harper, has also recognized the CCFTA to be an important phase in diversifying his country's exports and investments into emerging markets.

Nevertheless, not everyone is on board the "Virtuous Circle" locomotive. The FARC and ELN are not the only ones who would like to renegotiate the current economic model. For example, there is fear in many sectors of civil society that Colombia will not be able to sustain economic and social progress if the environment is wrecked, if the government practically gives away the country's precious resources to foreign corporations, and if such development strategies exacerbate poverty, inequality, violence, repression, worker exploitation, and displacement. Such concerns are not unfounded given Colombia's history *and* Canada's global reputation in the mining and energy sectors. For example, the results of a 2009 report commissioned by the Prospectors and Developers Association of Canada found Canadian companies in the mining sector to be four times more likely to violate tenets of corporate social and environmental responsibility than any other country.[262]

Canada's reputation is cause for alarm, especially considering the current state of Colombian security. Though the climate for investors and MNCs may be better in comparison to the 1990s, this does not mean the climate is better for Colombian citizens. Labor unions, NGOs, and civil groups have extensively documented how in the last decade Canadian companies have exacerbated existing conflicts: "It is estimated that these resource-rich regions [where Canadian companies are operating] are the source of 87% of forced displacements, 80% of violations of human rights and international humanitarian law, and 83% of assassinations of trade union leaders in the country."[263] Further, Canadian mining corporations lack regulatory mechanisms to make them accountable for the violations they commit on foreign soil. Attempts to pass legislation—such as Bill C-300 of 2010— have been defeated and recommended CSR frameworks—like the *2007 National Roundtable on Corporate Social Responsibility (CSR) and the Canadian Extractive Industry in Developing Countries*—have been neglected by the government.[264]

It is also worth noting that the two major insurgent movements have aligned to confront foreign corporations, especially those in the mining and energy sectors. On 31 March 2013, the leaderships of both the FARC and ELN sent the following communiqué:

> The political moment which the department of Arauca and Colombia's East is living through, merits all to reflect on the economic and social situation generated by the presence of the multinational companies and the disproportionate ambitions and the voracious appetite of the mining sector, which resulted in the region's militarization from which we suffer, breaking the environmental balance and tranquility of the entire society.[265]

Attacks against the oil sector by both groups have increased[266] and look to grow with the new alliance, which they are calling the "Popular Revolutionary Bloc":

> We call on the fighters, militants, all the revolutionaries of both forces, to assume with loyalty and dedication the unified Bolivarian spirit of our commanders Manuel Marulanda Velez and Manuel Perez Martinez, turning the pain into force; the challenge of today is to strengthen the Popular Revolutionary Bloc [to] confront the big oligopolies, transnational capital, and imperialism.[267]

With such advancement, we need to take special care when dealing with development amidst armed conflict to not further aggravate it.

Limits and opportunities of Colombian development

What was feared during the Cold War is also feared today—a top-down absolutist and universal "truth" forced upon a plural world where many identities, cultures, and civilizations exist. Fear during this era of globalization has caused many forms of resistance. As stated above, the armed resistances observed throughout Colombia's history can be assessed as counter-movements to the different violent challenges to traditional identities, interests, and social practices. Models forced upon a people tend to destroy the traditional cultural fabrics and coping mechanisms of society by forcing humans to be means to an end instead of ends in themselves. However, not all development strategies need to be top-down models, nor is force and coercion a necessary and sufficient condition for development and security.

Understanding Michel Foucault may better help conceptualize Colombian development and the armed conflict. For Foucault, knowledge was not *a priori* (reasoning based on theoretical deduction), but, rather, based on empirical observations and social practices, which, in turn, engendered "new concepts, and new techniques," along with "totally new forms of subjects and subjects of knowledge."[268] In this way, truth and knowledge do not reside within the subject, but amidst a backdrop of history because it is the subject that is entrenched in history and "is constantly established and reestablished in history."[269] With this as a foundation, it makes sense why Foucault posited that knowledge and truth were invented, had no origin, and were not inscribed into human nature. Knowledge and truth are directly attached to "pure and obscure power relations" connected to the configuration of political and social controls.[270] We can then understand the relationship between knowledge/truth/power and that which is supposedly known as arbitrary and socially constructed.[271] What gives rise to domains of knowledge are the social practices that survived as the outcome of an interplay, encounter, struggle, and compromise between power relations.[272] Truth is simply, for Foucault, an interpretation or perspective that has come into being as a "historical and circumstantial result of conditions outside the domain of knowledge"—of activity, not essence.[273] Knowledge and truth are, for Foucault, not a universal structure of content to be discovered, but, rather, invented and always given rise by the struggle for power.[274]

For Foucault, "truth isn't outside power or lacking in power," but of this world. This is important to understand when applying transformative practices. Acknowledging that every culture and society has a regime of truth allows for a battle for or around truth, "about the status of truth and the economic and political role it plays."[275] Regimes of truth are then subject to modifications because truth is directly connected with all techniques of power that exist to construct and secure it. These regimes are used to produce, organize, regulate, distribute, and operate statements that include or exclude from the norm.[276]

Foucault was right, power does not simply come from the top, but those in the bottom, too, have an influence and impact in how power relations operate. In this way, Foucault explained power to be cyclical, where those struggling to gain power can refuse the type of identities and subjectivities imposed on them by promoting new forms of subjectivity. In Colombia, the social forces of civil society exist, but have not been enacted to the point of becoming a strong enough wave to put out the wildfires of violence. James F. Rochlin was aware of the power of the people, and in *Social Forces and the Revolution in Military Affairs* he argued that

> civil society can empower itself through a clear understanding of the RMA, and can help shape the emerging revolution rather than being victimized by it at the hands of adversarial forces. There would be an emphasis, then, on the dimensions of human security associated with this rupture.[277]

However, the conventional Colombian understanding of power and hegemony can be summarized as follows. If a state can forcefully dominate the minds and actions of others to be able to accomplish its goals, then the state has more effective power in relation to those it is competing against for resources, security, and authority to achieve what it wants. Power in Colombia has been identified with coercion, not cooperation.

Others, however, like Foucault and the classical realists (Thucydides, Sun Tzu, Sun Tzu II, and Niccolò Machiavelli), suggested hegemony did not have to be defined this way. They informed that without the stronger making concessions to the weaker to win their consent, it is difficult to realize state aims. Without the consent of the governed—legitimacy—the state will be in a situation of constant fear of revolution, attack, and non-cooperation. In short, the non-consenting governed will make it difficult for the state to move forward and solidify its aims. Thus, a security policy primarily driven by force and coercion can be counter-productive since it creates an emotive, impassioned, and, at times, enraged opposition. They acknowledged that for a state to rid itself of anarchy and disorder, action would have to be based on taking into consideration the vulnerable and the weak. They saw a necessity for the state to be focused on the art of governing individuals to secure their permanent consent. Power, in turn, comes through cooperation and consent. In this way, the relative capacity to generate effective action in the world is increased.

What the leading actors in Colombia's armed conflict fear is not ideology per se (that which resides in the mind), but "the political, economic, institutional regime of the production of truth."[278] The struggle for truth is not necessarily emancipation from the social, economic, and cultural realms it currently maneuvers and functions, but to disengage its techniques of power "from the forms of hegemony."[279] In Colombia, the battle for truth has taken on this struggle to detach the current definition of truth that is supposed to be the authority on ethics and human interaction and transaction; a detachment from a capitalist epistemological interpretation of the world that Others a section of the population and instrumentalizes it to benefit a select few; not to mention a detachment from the tentacles of the Catholic Church. This struggle by guerrillas and part of civil society against the capitalist model embraces all three instruments of power while its most influential actors try to form obedient individuals for the sake of controlling minds, bodies, and resources.

Presently, we see examples of normalization and surveillance through terror—"physical fear, collective horror, images that must be engraved on the memories of spectators" through the use of force and coercion—and discipline based on collective reinforcements that illustrate "the link between the idea of crime and the idea of punishment." In the end, the goal is the same: to teach a lesson to control minds, bodies, and resources.[280] The human is subjected not solely to one person or a group of people, but to a system of power that increases the aptitude and capacity of everyone's docility for domination. For the system to be effective, it must minimize disturbances and maximize advantages, thereby producing a space where individuals all belong to a place and vice versa. The more knowledge is created about the individuals, the better the system can master and use people.[281] Discipline becomes the art of "composing forces to obtain an efficient machine" for the sake of normalization.[282] Colombia is still trying to fine-tune its instruments of power, and when the aim of having power of mind over mind—where the people can regulate themselves—and the increase of the docility of subjects and their utility are ineffective, terror is used to normalize.[283] Such terror has been epitomized by governments, paramilitaries, guerrillas, and exacerbated by MNCs. This "political economy of the body" is always situated in "the body and its forces, their utility and their docility, their distribution and their submission," as Foucault claimed.[284]

If development is to be sustainable and stable, if the drums of war are to be silenced, and healing is to begin, we need to discard and replace might-makes-right security principles with a more real and robust realism aligned to classical realist principles that take seriously the loose constellation of interrelated meanings that bind Colombians to each other. Consensual capacity building projects can have more lasting effects if a holistic approach toward development is desired, which takes into consideration economic growth simultaneously with environmental health and respect for human and labor rights. There are some in the Colombian military, such as Colonel Gabriel Pinilla, who understand this. Pinilla claimed the war cannot be won with purely military methods and suggested that

> it is necessary to implement strong economic measures, to establish generous and innovative alternatives, and implement other social models. Only by closing the inequality gap, will it be possible to put down the FARC's main justification, and find confidence in government intentions.[285]

We can also learn from Ann Mason's recommendation that if the "government is serious about winning the war by winning the hearts and minds of Colombian society, it must recognize that military progress against the FARC and paramilitaries is a necessary but insufficient condition for sustainable security, which is possible only with the implementation of the entire democratic security agenda."[286]

The Uribe-Santos Democratic Security and Defense Policy paved the way for the new economic boom, especially in the extractive sector, but it came at a cost. Democracy, human rights, and the environment were significantly violated by the government and others for the sake of profit. Such a pattern cannot continue if Colombia wishes to attain legitimacy and move away from a history of institutionalized violence and lacking hegemony that sets up the country for an uncertain, unstable, and unsustainable style of development. The historical underpinnings of Colombia's conflict resolution and development policies—from the Left to the Right—have proven counter-productive. We need to revise previous policies and models if Colombia and its people ever want to have the preconditions met not only for survival, but for the freedom to express their human potentials.

Since August of 2010, when Santos came into power, there has been further looking to dealing with the concerns of civil society, victims of violence, and to holding government institutions responsible. Peaceful, political conflict resolution strategies have also increased during his watch—with neighbors (Ecuador and Venezuela), civil society movements (e.g., the student movement), in victim recognition and reparation policies, with labor (e.g., coffee union), and, maybe most importantly, with the FARC. Colombia and Canada also signed the first FTA (Free Trade Agreement) with a side agreement that focuses on Human Rights Impact Assessments (HRIA). Though it is still early in this transition and the impacts of these new policy changes cannot be fully evaluated yet, it is a change in the right direction. Nevertheless, there is still more that can be done and needs to be done, especially in capacity building, human rights enforcement, Corporate Social and Environmental Responsibility, HRIAs, and accountability mechanisms that monitor and oversee government institutions and MNCs in Colombia.

How Institutions Stand in Colombians' Way

22 May 2012, *Colombia Reports*

I can't help but worry for the future of Colombia, and it's not a concern rooted in the conventionally accepted reasons for our violent strife. The way we raise and nurture our children is directly linked to why this armed conflict has yet to run out of breath. Our indoctrination and educational practices create generation after generation of ignorant masses. When faith is hailed as the highest virtue and history and scientific/philosophical thinking are rejected, *el pueblo* is easily deceived and exploited. Nevertheless, hope for a better tomorrow can be found in how we choose to deal with the decerebration of the masses.

The malady

Social structures and institutions put in place by the Catholic Church since Spanish colonial times and the government since the birth of the nation have steered Colombians into ignorance. Such mental poverty is directly linked to detrimental changes made to the education of our citizenry and the type of subjects the government and Catholicism have historically demanded of us. (90+ percent of Colombians self-identify as Catholic.) Both variables have been significantly influential for creating a cultural attitude and societal disposition that roll out the red carpet for conflict and/or fundamentalist practices.

For instance, it has been almost thirty years since the Ministry of Education removed History from the curriculum; thereby making Colombia one of the countries in the world that places the least amount of attention and effort into teaching history. Most history texts we do have are quite ancient and tend to hold a very Conservative bias since the large majority were written during the period regarded as the Conservative Hegemony. And let's not forget that most Colombians have been educated by the church. In 2005, for example, 81 percent of voters had been religiously educated, while the rest went through the public education system.

Further, if to be a member of an institution individuals must suspend reason and replace it with blind faith—as one is conditioned to do as a Colombian Catholic—then the direct result is a people who don't sincerely care if what they believe is true or factual. If they did care, they would demand higher levels of evidence and proof than, say, simply what they have been told is the word of God by preachers and the Bible.

We can extend this idea to the traditional two-party system of Colombia. Historically, Colombians have been born either Liberal or Conservative in the same way most are born into a religion. One was then indoctrinated—many still are—to toe the party line on faith as if it were a holy book, and to take the party leaders' words as holy orders by the high priests without question. Even in this century, we've seen this kind of polarizing dichotomy with the "you're either with us or you're with the terrorist" forms of rhetoric often flowing from the mouth of former President Álvaro Uribe Vélez.

The kind of individuals and collectives created by this ahistorical, blind-faith-praising cocktail puts us all in a complicated predicament. We become a society easily available for manipulation and herding. In a way, we are born and nurtured ready to be used as pawns for war or for helping create and perpetuate conditions for conflict. A country that neglects its history and suppresses its analytic faculties sacrifices its future and is more apt to repeat the worst moments of its past.

Is it any surprise violent and fundamentalist social practices are dominant? Is it any wonder that peaceful conflict resolution practices have widely been failures? If limited, distorted, or false beliefs and opinions are accepted as absolute truths, and such absolutes are taught to remain unquestioned and accepted on faith, it is no shock this relationship has been a hindrance to establishing lasting and enduring security and peace. A society that proclaims and imposes absolute truths—be it from religion or politics (capitalist vs. communist dogmas, for example)—sets the foundation for conflict.

It is not surprising that when Colombians themselves forward similar critiques as the one I am forwarding that they are not taken too seriously or are ostracized from society. Let us look at Piedad Cordoba and Ingrid Betancourt as examples. Cordoba's interpretation of the condition of Colombian culture is that the country is "absolutely blind and ignoring the cruel reality." Similarly, Betancourt has claimed, "There exists a species of 'consensus' in the country that obliges people to follow an opinion without questioning it."

Though these two women have been largely ostracized by mainstream media and administrations for different reasons, we should not reject everything they have said simply because we do not like the individuals who spoke. They have provided us with valuable insights that point to some of the major obstacles of the armed conflict. Constructing a fair and just society and resolving conflicts in a peaceful manner become difficult endeavors if the population is blind, ignoring the cruel reality, and, on faith, follow opinions without questioning them.

A modest proposal

For these reasons we must also unpack and dissect the frameworks of Colombian society—those lenses that pass as common sense—that are not sincerely questioned and/or effectively analyzed, and, as a result, may hinder the conflict resolution process. This is why we should also shine a spotlight on the roots of Colombian consciousness—its backdrop, social structures, agents, institutions, unspoken assumptions, and taken-for-granted ideologies—that make resolving conflicts a challenging enterprise. If not, as Ralph Waldo Emerson once said, "As long as a man stands in his own way, everything seems to be in his way."

All hope is not lost, however. There is still time to move out of our own way. We can begin by challenging and changing current institutions, social practices, and social structures.

As a start, I advance a modest proposal to (re)introduce the following three disciplines into the mandatory education system: (1) Philosophy, (2) World Religions, and (3) World and Colombian History.

First, philosophy would instill basic analytical and critical thinking skills that would aid in the process of safeguarding many from manipulation and exploitation. Education in philosophy would also help increase the demand for higher levels of evidence from not only our leaders but also from our very selves. One of the most common Colombian expressions provided as a response when people are asked to support their claims is "that's just what they say." This is indicative of a society run on unfounded assumptions and faulty opinions. There is a false notion that democracy means one person's ignorance is just as good as another person's knowledge. Such confused thinking results in an anemic and sick democracy. As the adage goes, just because you're entitled to your own opinion does not mean you're entitled to creating your own facts. Philosophical/scientific thinking helps reduce conflict by weeding out claims not grounded in reality, fact, or truth, and by providing an environment where well-informed and reasoned discussion and debate are favored over faith-based assertions.

Along with philosophy, a quest of world religions would introduce our youth to the different ways other cultures have historically answered the big existential questions. Not sheltering our children from other ways of thinking and ways of interpreting personal relationships with the self, others, nature, reality, and so on, can be quite conducive for co-existing peacefully in a plural world. The more we understand (or at least are open to understand) our surroundings and ourselves, the less fearful we will be of others and of specific situations. Lowered anxiety and fear tend to result in lowering the risk of conflict.

Lastly, a reintroduction of history into the educational repertoire helps prevent potential repetitions of previous conflicts. The better we are at gathering facts on the ground, the more effective we can be at describing, explaining, and predicting conflict. Such knowledge can then aid in constructing adequate strategies to tackle the direst issues facing Colombians today. It is difficult to deal with a conflict if we incorrectly interpret its causes, origins, and reasons for its existence. The more we know about our own history and the history of others, the better prepared we are for creating the lives we want to lead. The point is to learn from our past and the paths of others so we don't make the same mistakes.

Though there's a fine line between education and indoctrination, there are major distinctions worth highlighting. Indoctrination appeals to authority and suspends critical thinking. Education appeals to reason, fact, and logic. Indoctrination is often grounded on faith, which is the denial of observation so that belief can be preserved. Instead, the education I'm proposing is based on scientific and philosophical thinking that adjusts its views based on what's observed and tested.

If the latter is rejected and the former embraced, conflict is almost sure to surface. If those engaged in conflict do not care about knowledge or facts—if they do not even care if what they themselves believe is true (yet they believe their interpretation of reality to be an absolute truth)—then resolving conflict peacefully becomes laborious.

We should not be so eager to spit on our ancestors or push each other off the shoulders of the great giants who got us this far. It is not too late to move out of our own way.

About the Author

Julián Esteban Torres López is a Colombian-born journalist, publisher, podcaster, and editor. Before founding the nonfiction storytelling organization *The Nasiona*, he ran several cultural and arts organizations, edited journals and books, was a social justice and public history researcher, wrote a column for *Colombia Reports*, taught university courses, and managed a history museum. He's a Pushcart Prize and Best Small Fictions nominee and has written two books on social justice. Torres López holds a bachelor's in philosophy and in communication and a master's in justice studies from University of New Hampshire and was a Ph.D. candidate at University of British Columbia Okanagan, where he focused on political science and Latin American studies.

jetorreslopez.com

Acknowledgments

If I have seen further, it is by standing on the shoulders of giants.

Issac Newton.

My most humble thanks to the following four renown thinkers and professionals, without whom I probably would not have had the opportunities to learn about the world in the manner I did: Nick Smith, Joshua Meyrowitz, James Rochlin, and Adriaan Alsema. I introduce them in the order I first met them. I am grateful to:

Nick Smith (Professor of Philosophy and Justice Studies, University of New Hampshire), for opening my eyes to the many realms of the human condition through philosophy. As my professor, advisor, and thesis director, he helped me explore the arts, law, ethics, politics, and issues of justice. Not only did he introduce me to fundamental questions about the internal and external world—which still linger, as I consider them some of the most important questions ever asked of me—but he taught me how to become a better student, writer, and person. He helped me explore concerns that ultimately led to my desire to further understand my identity, place in the world, and Colombian power relations. His teaching style and intellectual rigor is what I, to this day, try to emulate.

Joshua Meyrowitz (retired Professor of Communication, University of New Hampshire), for opening my eyes to how technologies, especially communication technologies, have shaped and influenced social relations we encounter daily. His media analysis and criticism helped me become cautious and prudent about information and news sources, as well as learn how variables can be manipulated to distract from or enhance a message. I took one of his university courses twice simply because I felt the material he taught was that important, and I wanted to steep in it longer to better grasp it. He was the first to give me the opportunity to academically explore the role of the United States in Colombia.

James F. Rochlin (Professor of Political Science, University of British Columbia Okanagan), for taking me under his wing and helping me understand the world—and Colombia, specifically—through the lens of a first-rate professor and political scientist. As my Ph.D. program supervisor and professor, he provided me with the kind of education, support, and opportunities any graduate student would ever want to receive. He taught me through dialogue, walks, analysis, friendship, feedback, and hands-on field work, along with introducing me to the nuanced and complex discourses of my fields: political science, Latin American studies, and Colombia's armed conflict.

Adriaan Alsema, founder and director of *Colombia Reports* (Colombia's largest independent news source in English), for giving me the opportunity to write a column on Colombia's history, culture, peoples, and armed conflict over the course of 2010 to 2012. I was fortunate not only for the column, but also to be involved in the newsroom. His authentic curiosity for facts and truth, accuracy, humanity, journalistic integrity, and analytical mind made me a better writer and thinker. After being disillusioned with the state of Colombian journalism for so many years, this intimate experience with *Colombia Reports* was refreshing.

All these individuals lead by example, and I recognize a little part of them in every endeavor I undertake. They have given me a clear picture of what I should aim to become as a researcher, thinker, and journalist, and the kind of work and dedication needed to succeed in my professional and creative life activities. They also treated me with compassion and benevolence, dedicating endless hours to help a budding student of the world develop. I owe a lot of who I am today to these men.

By standing upon the shoulders of these giants, I have a greater sense of place and a better view of the world. Thank you for propping me up.

Endnotes

[1] Bolívar, Simón. *El Libertador: Writings of Simón Bolívar*. Trans. Frederick H. Fornoff. Oxford: Oxford University Press, 2003. 48.

[2] James F. Rochlin, *Social Forces and the Revolution in Military Affairs: The Cases of Colombia and Mexico*, Manuscript before publication, 2007 copy. See also James F. Rochlin, "Who Said the Cold War is Over? The political economy of strategic conflict between Venezuela and Colombia," *Third World Quarterly*, Vol. 32, No. 2, 2011, pp 237-260.

[3] Bert Ruiz. 2001. *The Colombian civil war*. London: McFarland & Company.

[4] Charles Bergquist. 2001. Waging war and negotiating peace: The contemporary crisis in historical perspective. In *Violence in Colombia 1990-2001:Waging war and negotiating peace*, eds. Charles Bergquist, Ricardo Penaranda, and Gonzalo Sanchez, pp. 1-26. Wilmington, DE: Scholarly Resources, Inc. See also Charles Bergquist. 1978. *Coffee and conflict in Colombia, 1886-1910*. Durham, NC: Duke University Press.

[5] Jenny Pearce. 1990. *Colombia: Inside the labyrinth*. London: Latin American Research Bureau.

[6] Alex McDougall, "State Power and Its Implications for Civil War Colombia," *Studies in Conflict & Terrorism*, 32: 322-345, 2009.

[7] Paramilitary/neo-paramilitary organizations, FARC, and ELN.

[8] Alex McDougall, "State Power and Its Implications for Civil War Colombia," *Studies in Conflict & Terrorism*, 32: 322-345, 2009. Pp. 340-341.

[9] Colombia is divided by three major mountain ranges, bordering two oceans, the Amazon jungle, among other physical impediments.

[10] Bolívar, 6.

[11] Bolívar, 25.

[12] Bolívar, 25, 27.

[13] Bolívar, 47.

[14] Bolívar, 61.

[15] Bolívar, 40.

[16] Bolívar, 60.

[17] Bolívar, 93.

[18] Bolívar, 94.

[19] Bolívar, 48.

[20] Bolívar, 88.

[21] Bolívar, 7, 8.

[22] Bolívar, 8.

[23] Bolívar, 90-91.

[24] Bolívar, 101.

[25] Bolívar, 58.

[26] Schlessinger Video Productions, *Simón Bolívar: Latin-American Revolutionary* (Bala Cynwyd, PA: Schlessinger Video Productions, 1995). [videorecording]

[27] Carlos Fuentes, *The Buried Mirror: Reflections on Spain and the New World* (New York: First Mariner Books, 1999), 277.

[28] Fuentes, 286.

[29] Fuentes, 264.

[30] Such as water, oil, gas, illicit drugs, and mining resources.

[31] Public Workshop. "Colombia, the Conflicts and Beyond: Perspectives on a Canadian Ally," Simon Fraser University, Segal School of Business, Event Rooms 1300-1500, 500 Granville St. Vancouver, BC, Canada, 19 April 2009, <http://www.sfu.ca/las/news/ColombiaTheConflictsandBeyond.html>

[32] David Bushnell, *The Making of Modern Colombia: A Nation in Spite of Itself* (Los Angeles: University of California, 1993), 151. Charles Bergquist, *Coffee and Conflict in Colombia, 1886-1910* (Durham, N.C., 1978), 145.

[33] Having the state, not the church, control education, for example.

[34] Gran Colombia was the original republic post-liberation and it encompassed present-day Venezuela, Ecuador, Panama, and parts of Costa Rica, Guyana, Nicaragua, Peru, and Brazil.

[35] Sebastián Mazzuca & James A. Robinson, "Political Conflict and Power Sharing in the Origins of Modern Colombia," *Hispanic American Historical Review*, 89:2, p. 286.

[36] Mazzuca & Robinson, 288.

[37] Bonifacio Vélez, *Proyecto de ley sobre reforma electoral* (Bogotá: Imprenta Nacional, 1905), 69-70.

[38] Carlos Martínez Silva, *Revistas políticas publicadas en el repertorio* (Bogotá: Imprenta Nacional, 1934), 2: pp. 467-68, 500-501. Se also *Anales de la Cámera de Representantes*, 1898, p. 387.

[39] Rafael Uribe Uribe's speech can be found in *Anales de la Cámera de Representantes*, 1898, p 390. This particular translation is by Sebastián Mazzuca and James A. Robinson.

[40] See Mazzuca and Robinson for more on this topic.

[41] Hannah Arendt, *On Violence* (Harcourt Books, 1970), 56.

[42] In comparison to the near one-hundred per cent monopoly of the Conservatives during the last decades of the 19th century.

[43] Many would claim that the U.S. did come to control Colombia through its many policies and aid, such as the U.S. Containment policy during the cold war, drug war, war on terror, Plan Colombia, 2009 military bases agreement, and trade agreements, among others.

[44] Boyer, Clark, Hawley, Kett, Rieser, Salisbury, Sitkoff, and Woloch, *The Enduring Vision: A History of the American People, Volume 2: Since 1865* (Boston: Wadsworth Cengage Learning, 2010), 508.

[45] Eduardo Galeano,*Open Veins of Latin America: Five Centuries of the Pillage of a Continent* (New York: Monthly Review Press, 1997), 107-108. Noam Chomsky, *Turning the Tide: U.S. Intervention in Central America and the Struggle for Peace* (Boston: South End Press, 1987), 59.

[46] United Fruit Historical Society, "1928," < http://www.unitedfruit.org/chron.htm >

[47] Telegram from the Bogotá Embassy to the U.S. Secretary of State, 5 December 1928 <http://www.icdc.com/~paulwolf/colombia/santamarta.htm>

[48] Telegram from the Bogotá Embassy to the U.S. Secretary of State, 7 December 1928, <http://www.icdc.com/~paulwolf/colombia/santamarta.htm>

[49] Telegram from the U.S. Department of State to the Santa Marta Consulate, 8 December 1928, <http://www.icdc.com/~paulwolf/colombia/santamarta.htm>

[50] Telegram from the Santa Marta Consulate to the U.S. Secretary of State, 6 December 1928, <http://www.icdc.com/~paulwolf/colombia/santamarta.htm>

[51] Telegram from the Santa Marta Consulate to the U.S. Secretary of State, 8 December 1928, <http://www.icdc.com/~paulwolf/colombia/santamarta.htm>

[52] Dispatch from the U.S. Bogotá Embassy to the U.S. Secretary of State, 16 January 1929, <http://www.icdc.com/~paulwolf/colombia/santamarta.htm>

[53] Galeano, 103.

[54]Herbert Braun, *Our Guerrillas, Our Sidewalks: A Journey into the Violence of Colombia* (Niwot, C.O.: University Press of Colorado, 1994), 9.

[55] Daniel Pécault, *Las FARC: ¿una guerrilla sin fin or sin fines?* (Bogotá: Grupo Editorial Norma, 2008), 31-32.

[56] James D. Henderson, *When Colombia Bled: A History of the Violence in Tolima* (Tuscaloosa: University of Alabama Press, 1985), 222.

[57] Manuel Marulanda Vélez, "The Republic of Marquetalia-Manifesto, issued July 20, 1964, by the Revolutionary Armed Forces of Colombia, FARC," in J. Gerasso, ed., *The Coming of the New International*, New York: The World Publishing Company, 1971, pp. 502-503.

[58] FARC Secretariat of the Central Staff, "36 Years for Peace and National Sovereignty."

[59] FARC Secretariat of the Central Staff, "36 Years for Peace and National Sovereignty."

[60] FARC Secretariat of the Central Staff, "36 Years for Peace and National Sovereignty."

[61] Gomez-Suarez, Andrei, "Perpetrator blocs, genocidal mentalities and geographies: the destruction of the Union Patriotica in Colombia and its lessons for genocide studies," *Journal of Genocide Research* (2007), 9 (4), December, 637.

[62] FARC Secretariat of the Central Staff, "36 Years for Peace and National Sovereignty."

[63] Andrés Pastrana & Camilo Gomez, *La Palabra bajo Fuego* (Bogota: Editorial Planeta Colombiana S.A., 2005), 48-51.

[64] Grace Livingstone (2004). *Inside Colombia: Drugs, Democracy, and War* (Rutgers University Press), 123-130.

[65] As Marta Lucía Ramírez stated a few months before becoming Uribe's Defense Minister in 2003. *El Tiempo*. Bogotá, junio 16 de 2003, p. 1A.

[66] *BBC Mundo*, "Colombia en emergencia," 12 de agosto de 2002, <http://news.bbc.co.uk/hi/spanish/latin_america/newsid_2187000/2187 676.stm>

[67] Stockholm International Peace Research Institute, The SIPRI Military Expenditure Database, "Colombia, <http://milexdata.sipri.org/result.php4>

[68] Over $5 billion from the U.S. alone during Uribe's tenure, and Colombia itself $8 billion since the implementation of Plan Colombia a decade ago. Colombia is the largest recipient of U.S. military aid in the hemisphere, and up to the start of the Iraq invasion Colombia was the third largest recipient in the world after Israel and Egypt. Around 70-80% of U.S. Plan Colombia funding went to militarizing Colombia.

[69] Ushma Patel, "Revealing the benefits of Colombian drug legalization," Princeton University News, 19 April 2010, <http://www.princeton.edu/main/news/archive/S27/14/23G46/index.x ml?section=featured>

[70] For a deeper analysis, see Rojas, 28.

[71] *CaracolTV*, "El legado que Uribe déjà a su successor," 26 mayo 2010, <http://www.caracoltv.com/noticias/politica/articulo-179346-el-legado-uribe-deja-a-su-sucesor>

[72] For example, in 2007-2008, 76 percent of Plan Colombia's budget was devoted to the military and police. See *World Politics Review* (15 Feb 2007). Also see *Just the Facts (a civilian's guide to U.S. defense*

and security assistance to Latin America and the Caribbean), "U.S. Aid to Colombia, <http://justf.org/Country?country=Colombia>

[73] Colombian Ministry of Defense, "Virtuous Circle," Annual Report.

[74] BBC. "Uribe defends security policies." *BBC News*. 18 Nov. 2004. <http://news.bbc.co.uk/2/hi/americas/4021213.stm>

[75] Hernández, Álvaro. "Uribe pide a E.U. un despliegue military en Colombia 'similar' al de Irak." *Agencia de Noticias de Informacion Alternativa*. 21 Jan. 2003.

[76] For Uribe, hegemony meant dominance and control.

[77] Simón Bolívar, *El Libertador: Writings of Simón Bolívar*. Trans. Frederick H. Fornoff (Oxford: Oxford University Press, 2003), 13, 15.

[78] Bolívar, 125.

[79] Bolívar, 52, 144.

[80] Bolívar, 116.

[81] Bolívar, 10.

[82] *El Tiempo*, "Juan Manuel Santos aseguró que Uribe 'fue un Segundo Libertador' para Colombia," 6 de agosto de 2010, <http://www.eltiempo.com/colombia/politica/presidente-electo-juan-manuel-santos-se-convirtio-en-gran-maestro-_7844925-1>

[83] American Jewish Committee, "President Uribe receives AJC Light unto the Nations Award," 4 May 2007, <http://www.ajc.org/site/apps/nl/content2.asp?c=ijITI2PHKoG&b=153 1911&ct=3841031>

[84] *The Huffington Post*, "Bush Chooses Uribe, Blair, Howard For Medal of Freedom," 5 January 2009, <http://www.huffingtonpost.com/2009/01/05/bush-chooses-uribe-blair-_n_155435.html>

[85] Philip J. Crowley, "Daily Press Briefing," U.S. Department of State, 2 August 2010, <http://www.state.gov/r/pa/prs/dpb/2010/08/145491.htm>

[86] *El Espectador*, "Uribe sera premiado en España por el apoyo a víctimas del terrorismo," 6 septiembre 2010, <http://www.elespectador.com/noticias/paz/articulo-222797-uribe-sera-premiado-espana-el-apoyo-victimas-del-terrorismo>

[87] Embassy of Colombia (Washington). "The Uribe Administration's Security and Defense Policy." Embassy of Colombia, Washington, D.C. <http://www.presidencia.gov.co/sne/visita_bush/documentos/security.pdf>

[88] Jorge Torres, "Crimen organizado creciógracias a élites mexicanas," *El Universal*, 27 de febrero 2010, <http://www.eluniversal.com.mx/primera/34503.html>

[89] Statistics from Escuala Nacional Sindical.

[90] *Caracol TV*, "El legado que Uribe déjà a su successor," 26 mayo 2010," <http://www.caracoltv.com/noticias/politica/articulo-179346-el-legado-uribe-deja-a-su-sucesor>

[91] National Defense Ministry, Annual Report.

[92] *TeleSur*, "Uribe se pronunció en torno a fallo de ex coronel Plazas," junio 10 de 2010.

[93] U.S. Office of National Drug Control Policy, "Source Countries and Drug Transit Zones: Colombia," <http://www.whitehousedrugpolicy.gov/international/colombia.html>

[94] U.S. Office of National Drug Control Policy, "Source Countries and Drug Transit Zones: Colombia," <http://www.whitehousedrugpolicy.gov/international/colombia.html>

[95] See Amnesty International's annual reports on Colombia.

---

[96] Though this scandal only unfolded into the mass public sphere in October of 2008, documents have arisen stating that in Colombia, at least as far back as 1990, there has been an institutional incentive to take the lives of the very people the security forces supposed to protect. It was also around this same time that the U.S. Embassy in Colombia began to see connections between Colombia's military and paramilitary (National Security Archive. George Washington University, DC. 1990. <http://www.gwu.edu/~nsarchiv/colombia/19900727.pdf>).

In 1994, the issue was not dead and it was concluded that "body count mentalities" were widespread among those seeking promotion in the Army and that security forces were employing "death squad tactics in their counterinsurgency campaign." It was concluded that Colombia had a "history of assassinating leftwing civilians in guerrilla areas" (National Security Archive. 1994. <http://www.gwu.edu/~nsarchiv/colombia/19941021.pdf>). High-ranking military officials have since come out claiming, as one General did, that this body count mentality "tends to fuel human rights abuses by well-meaning soldiers trying to get their quota to impress superiors. It could also lead to a cavalier, or at least passive, approach when it comes to allowing the paramilitaries to serve as proxies for the [Colombian Army] in contributing to the guerrilla body count" (National Security Archive. 1997. <http://www.nsarchive.org/colombia/19971224.pdf>). In 2000 the U.S. Embassy reported that there was clear evidence of "Army-paramilitary complicity" thereby directly tying the Colombian military to the paramilitary in the opportunity to increase the body count in combat, regardless if the individuals assassinated were actually rebels or not (National Security Archive. 2000. <http://www.nsarchive.org/colombia/20000208.pdf>).

[97] Vincent Bevins, "Another scandal gets dodged," *New Statesman*, 2 July 2009, <http://www.newstatesman.com/world-affairs/2009/07/colombia-uribe-military-FARC>

[98] Constanza Vieira, "COLOMBIA: UN Confirms 'Systematic' Killings of Civilians by Soldiers," IPS, 19 June 2009, <http://www.ipsnews.net/news.asp?idnews=47300>

[99] *Caracol Radio*, "ONU cuestiona el pago de recompensas en Colombia para enfrentar la lucha contra la guerrilla," Julio 16 de 2010, <http://www.caracol.com.co/nota.aspx?id=1328160>

[100] Colonel Gabriel Pinilla (Colombian Army), "Are we approaching the real defeat of the FARC?" US War College, International Fellow, Class of 2009. Master's of Strategic Studies Strategy Research Project, p.19.

[101] *Caracol TV*, "Ordenan capturer a siete militares por 'falso positivo' en Sucre," 1 septiembre 2010, 'http://www.caracoltv.com/noticias/justicia/articulo-188837-ordenan-capturar-a-siete-militares-falso-positivo-sucre

[102] Vieira, <http://www.ipsnews.net/news.asp?idnews=47300>

[103] Adriaan Alsema, "Progress on the false positives cases: a case of false hope?" *Colombia Reports*, 15 January 2010, <http://colombiareports.com/opinion/the-colombiamerican/7686-progress-on-the-false-positives-cases-just-a-case-of-false-hope.html>

[104] Constanza Vieira, "COLOMBIA: UN Confirms 'Systematic' Killings of Civilians by Soldiers," IPS, 19 June 2009, <http://www.ipsnews.net/news.asp?idnews=47300>

[105] Amnesty International Report on Colombia, 2008.

[106] *El Espectador*, "Denuncian más de 3 mil ejecusiones extrajudiciales entre 2002 y 2009," 24 mayo 2010, <http://www.elespectador.com/ejecuciones-extrajudiciales/articulo-204807-colombia-hubo-mas-de-3-mil-ejecuciones-extrajudiciales-e>

[107] "Report: Military Assistance and human Rights: Colombia, U.S. Accountability, and Global Implications," *The Fellowship of Reconciliation*, <http://forusa.org/content/report-military-assistance-human-rights-colombia-us-accountability-global-implications>

[108] Coalition for the International Criminal Court, "ICC Background Paper," 20 May 2010, p4, <http://www.iccnow.org/documents/CICC_Review_Conference_Background_Paper.pdf>

[109] *El Espectador*, "Uribe propondrá blindar a Fuerza Pública de acciones jurídicas," 10 junio de 2010, <http://www.elespectador.com/articulo-207741-uribe-convoca-los-altos-mando-militares-analizar-condena-plazas-vega>

[110] *TeleSur*, "Uribe se pronunció en torno a fallo de ex coronel Plazas," junio 10 de 2010.

[111] Michael Solis, "Colombia's Internally Displaced People," *Huffington Post*, 13 September 2010, < http://www.huffingtonpost.com/michael-solis/colombias-internally-disp_b_715186.html>

[112] Codhes, 2010.

[113] Adriaan Alsema, "More than 10% of Colombians are displaced: court," *Colombia Reports*, 2 September 2010, <http://www.colombiareports.com/colombia-news/news/11652-more-than-10-of-colombians-is-displaced-court.html>

[114] Territory is also valuable for strategic military purposes.

[115] Codhes, Consultoría para los derechos humanos y el desplazamiento.

[116] John Otis, "If Colombia Is Winning Its War, Why the Fleeing?" *Time*, 1 September 2010, <http://www.time.com/time/world/article/0,8599,1919758,00.html?xid=rss-topstories>

[117] Margarita Rodriguez, "Biocombustibles en Colombia, ¿a que precio?," *BBC Mundo*, Junio 3 de 2009, <http://www.bbc.co.uk/mundo/america_latina/2009/06/090602_1855_biocombustibles_colombia_mr.shtml>

[118] *Cambio*, "El pais segun Jose Obdulio," Agosto 13 de 2008, <http://www.cambio.com.co/portadacambio/789/ARTICULO-PRINTER_FRIENDLY-PRINTER_FRIENDLY_CAMBIO-4445405.html>

[119] *Far Worse than Watergate*, Washington Office on Latin America, U.S. Office on Colombia, Latin America Working groupd, and teh Center for International Policy, 17 June 2010, <http://www.wola.org/index.php?option=com_content&task=viewp&id=1121&Itemid=33>

[120] Amnesty International, "Colombia: Paramilitary infiltration of state institutions undermines rule of law," 29 November 2006, <http://www.amnestyusa.org/document.php?lang=e&id=ENGAMR230482006>

[121] Hannah Stone, "HRW report 'distorts reality': Ministry of Defense," *Colombia Reports*, 3 February 2010, <http://colombiareports.com/colombia-news/news/8023-hrw-report-distorts-reality-ministry-of-defense.html> . Hannah Stone, "'Paramilitarism is extinct': Govt rejects HRW report," *Colombia Reports*, 4 February 2010, <http://colombiareports.com/colombia-news/news/8040-paramilitarism-is-extinct-govt-rejects-hrw-report.html>

[122] Numan Rights Watch, "Paramiiltaries' Heirs: The New Face of Violence in Colombia," 3 February 2010, <http://www.hrw.org/node/88060> Also, for a detailed history of paramilitarism and neo-paramilitarism in Colombia, refer to Jasmin Hristov's *Blood and Capital: The Paramilitarization of Colombia*.

[123] *Caracol TV*, "Preocupa índice de desmovilizados que vuelven a delinquir," Bogotá, 25 julio 2010, <http://www.caracoltv.com/desmovilizados/articulo-184851-preocupa-indice-de-desmovilizados-vuelven-a-delinquir>

[124] Amnesty International, *Amnesty International Report 2010 - Colombia*, 28 May 2010, p.110, <http://thereport.amnesty.org/sites/default/files/AIR2010_AZ_EN.pdf#page=55>

[125] *Semana*, "'Juicio' histórioa en Mampuján," 24 de abril de 2010, <http://www.semana.com/noticias-nacion/juicio-historico-mampujan/138041.aspx>

[126] *El Tiempo*, "Ya son 45 los líderes de víctimas asesinados por reclamar sus tierras; en 15 días murieron tres," Bogotá, 3 de junio de 2010, <http://www.eltiempo.com/colombia/justicia/ya-son-45-los-lideres-de-victimas-asesinados-por-reclamar-sus-tierras_7737280-1>

[127] *El Tiempo*, "Ya son 45 los líderes de víctimas asesinados por reclamar sus tierras; en 15 días murieron tres," Bogotá, 3 de junio de 2010, <http://www.eltiempo.com/colombia/justicia/ya-son-45-los-lideres-de-victimas-asesinados-por-reclamar-sus-tierras_7737280-1>

[128] Primo Levi, *The Drowned and the Saved* (New York: Vintage International, 1989), 200.

[129] *El Tiempo*, "Este jueves termina el tiempo para que víctimas del conflict reclamen indemnizaciones del Estado," Bogotá, 22 de abril de 2010, <http://www.eltiempo.com/colombia/justicia/termina-plazo-para-que-victimas-reclamen-indemnizaciones_7642524-1>

[130] Jasmin Hristov, *Blood and Capital: The Paramilitarization of Colombia*, (Toronto: Between the Lines, 2009), Chapter 5, 128-178.

[131] Hristov, 148.

[132] Hristov, 162

[133] Carlos Olimpo Restrepo S., "Por Justicia y Paz se difieren extradiciones," *El Colombiano*, Medellín, 29 junio de 2010, <http://www.elcolombiano.com/BancoConocimiento/P/por_justicia_y_paz_se_difieren_extradiciones/por_justicia_y_paz_se_difieren_extradiciones.asp>

[134] *Caracol Radio*, "Uribe defiende la extradición de los jefes paramilitares," mayo 4 de 2010, <http://www.caracol.com.co/nota.aspx?id=1019068>

[135] *Caracol TV*, "Calculan en 1500.000 los casos de ejecuciones extrajudiciales en Colombia," 22 abril 2010, < http://caracoltv.com/node/176099>

[136] *Caracol*, "No hay dinero para investigar crímenes de 'paras' ni para modernización," 24 agosto 2010, <http://www.caracol.com.co/nota.aspx?id=1348245>

[137] See María Camila López Rojas,"Efectos de la Regionalización de la Política de Seguridad Democrática: para el desplazamiento en las fronteras de Colombia," *Colombia Internacional* 65, ene - iun 2007, pp. 136 -151.

[138] Codhes, "Más o menos Deplazados," *Boletín de la Consultoría para los Derechos Humanos y el Desplazamiento*, No. 69, Bogotá-Colombia, 12 de septiembre 2006, p3.

[139] Codhes, 15.

[140] Codhes, 2010.

[141] *El Espectador*, "Más de 600 mil colombianos abandonarían el país en 2010," 5 enero 2010, <http://elespectador.com/noticias/judicial/articulo180559-mas-de-600-mil-colombianos-abandonarian-el-pais-2010>

[142] Charlie Devereux, "Venezuela vs. Colombia: The Battle Over Emigrés," *Time*, 5 November 2009, <http://www.time.com/time/world/article/0,8599,1934326,00.html>

[143] López Rojas, 144.

[144] Brian Ellsworth, "Venezuela border violence remains after crisis," *Reuters*, 18 March 2008, <http://uk.reuters.com/article/idUKN0564070720080318>

[145] Damon Barrett, "Update: Ecuador v Colombia, International Court of Justice," *International Centre on Human Rights and Drug Policy*, 17 August 2010, <http://www.humanrightsanddrugs.org/?p=1161>

[146] Adriaan Alsema, "Colombia to conduct aerial fumigation on Venezuela border," *Colombia Reports*, 13 March 2009, <http://colombiareports.com/colombia-news/news/3213-colombia-to-conduct-aerial-fumigation-on-venezuela-border.html>

[147] *El Tiempo*, "FBI tuvo 'chuzados' teléfonos de varios cabecillas de las FARC," 19 febrero 2008, <http://www.eltiempo.com/archivo/documento/CMS-3964744>

[148] Organization of American States, "Convocation of the meeting of consultation of Ministers of Foreign Affairs and appointment of a commission," 5 March 2008, <http://www.reliefweb.int/rw/RWB.NSF/db900SID/SHES-7CHSS4?OpenDocument>

[149] *Ecuador Inmediato*, "Si Quito hubiera cooperado, la incursion se habría evitado", dice ministro de Defensa colombiano, 3 marzo 2008, <http://www.ecuadorinmediato.com/Noticias/news_user_view/_quotsi_quito_hubiera_cooperado_la_incursion_se_habria_evitado_quot_dice_ministro_de_defensa_colombiano--72734>

[150] Author conversation with U.S. Consulate General, Philip Chicola, University of British Columbia Okanagan, Kelowna, Thursday, September 30, 2010.

[151] *Semana*, "Uribe atribuye desempleo en Colombia a crisis mundial y tension con Venezuela," 2 julio 2010, <http://www.semana.com/noticias-economia/uribe-atribuye-desempleo-colombia-crisis-mundial-tension-venezuela/141173.aspx>

[152] Original May 2009 leaked U.S. Air Force document, <http://www.centrodealerta.org/documentos_desclasificados/original_in_english_air_for.pdf>. Eva Golinger, "Military Coverup:Washington alters US Air Force document to hide intentions behind military accord with Colombia," *Global Research: Centre for Research on Globalization*, 28 November 2009, <http://www.globalresearch.ca/index.php?context=va&aid=16308>

[153] Modified U.S. Air Force document, 16 November 2009, <http://www.centrodealerta.org/noticias/ultima_hora_washington_alte.html>

[154] Philip J. Crowley, Assistant Secretary, U.S. Government, "Daily Press Briefing," 16 July 2010, <http://www.state.gov/r/pa/prs/dpb/2010/07/144770.htm>

[155] *PressTV*, "Bolivia calls for South American summit," 25 July 2010, <http://edition.presstv.ir/detail/136126.html>

[156] Gustavo Bell, Sandra Borda, Hernando José Gómez, Socorro Ramírez, Mauricio Reina, Camilo Reyes, Juan Gabriel Tokatlian, "Misión de Política Exterior de Colombia," Fedesarrollo, Gobierno de Colombia, April 2010, <http://web.presidencia.gov.co/sp/2010/abril/16/mision_politica_exterior.pdf>

[157] Vicepresidencia de la Republica de Colombia, "Gobierno firma memorando de entendimiento con el Instituto Interamericano de Derechos Humanos," 4 octubre 2010, <http://www.vicepresidencia.gov.co/Noticias/2010/Paginas/101004b.aspx>

[158] Presidencia de la Republica de Colombia, "'Urna de Cristal sera la revolución de la participación ciudadana': Presidente Santos," 6 octubre 2010, <http://wsp.presidencia.gov.co/Prensa/2010/Octubre/Paginas/20101006_06.aspx>

[159] Javier Darío Restrepo, "Land Reform, a top Priority of New Colombian Government," *Inter Press Service News Agency (IPS)*, 4 October 2010, <http://www.ipsnews.net/news.asp?idnews=53048>; *CaracolTV*, "Santos pide al Congreso aprobar la ley de tierras," 4 septiembre 2010, <http://www.caracoltv.com/noticias/politica/video-191741-presidente-santos-radica-persona-proyecto-de-ley-de-victimas?utm_source=Twitter+Feed&utm_medium=twitter>

[160] *El Colombiano*, "Presidente Santos reiteró compromise de construer un millón de viviendas," 4 septiembre 2010, <http://www.elcolombiano.com/BancoConocimiento/P/presidente_santos_reitero_compromiso_de_construir_un_milon_de_viviendas/presidente_santos_reitero_compromiso_de_construir_un_milon_de_viviendas.asp?CodSeccion=182>

[161] *Al Jazeera*, "US-Colombia pact 'unconstitutional,'" 18 August 2010, <http://english.aljazeera.net/news/americas/2010/08/20108180576316934.html>

[162] *El Espectador*, "Santos analizará si envía al Congreso acuerdo con EE.UU." 18 agosto 2010, <http://elespectador.com/articulo-219735-santos-dice-cooperacion-eeuu-no-se-va-suspender>

[163] Adriaan Alsema, "Cordoba dismissed for 'promoting and collaborating with' FARC: IG," 27 September 2010, <http://www.colombiareports.com/colombia-news/news/12068-cordoba-suspended-for-promoting-and-collaborating-with-FARC-ig.html>

[164] *RCN*, "Santos radicó Ley de víctimas," 27 septiembre 2010, <http://www.canalrcnmsn.com/noticias/santos_radic%C3%B3_ley_de_v%C3%ADctimas>; *TeleSur*, "Senado colombiano pide reconocer a víctimas de crímenes de Estado," 2 septiembre 2010, <http://multimedia.telesurtv.net/2/9/2010/15309/senado-colombiano-pide-reconocer-a-victimas-de-crimenes-de-estado/>

[165] *Caracol Radio*, "Ex presidents entregaron apoyo absolute a estrategia de Colombia con Ecuador y Venezuela," 5 octubre 2010, < http://www.caracol.com.co/nota.aspx?id=1366982>

[166] *Semana*, "Cómo sera la política exterior de Santos," 6 agosto 2010, <http://www.semana.com/noticias-politica/como-sera-politica-exterior-santos/142266.aspx>

[167] Gonzalo Ortiz, "Ecuador's Open Door Begins to Close for Some," *IPS*, 10 September 2010, <http://ipsnews.net/news.asp?idnews=52790>

[168] *Semana*, "Ecuador tiene esperanza de retomar relaciones con Colombia antes de diciembre," 2 septiembre 2010, <http://www.semana.com/noticias-politica/ecuador-tiene-esperanza-retomar-relaciones-colombia-antes-diciembre/143901.aspx>

[169] *Reuters/EP*, "Un juez revoca la order de prisión contra Santos por el bombardeo a un campamento de las FARC," 30 agosto 2010, < http://www.europapress.es/latam/politica/noticia-colombia-ecuador-juez-revoca-orden-prision-contra-santos-bombardeo-campamento-FARC-20100830191920.html>

[170] *Caracol Radio*, "Ex presidents entregaron apoyo absolute a estrategia de Colombia con Ecuador y Venezuela," 5 octubre 2010, < http://www.caracol.com.co/nota.aspx?id=1366982>

[171] Constanza Vieira and Helda Martínez, "Santos Inherits Country of Economic Contrasts," 9 August 2010, <http://ipsnews.net/news.asp?idnews=52434>

[172] *Semana*, "Ecuador tiene esperanza de retomar relaciones con Colombia antes de diciembre," 2 septiembre 2010, <http://www.semana.com/noticias-politica/ecuador-tiene-esperanza-retomar-relaciones-colombia-antes-diciembre/143901.aspx>

[173] *El Espectador*, "Colombia y Ecuador se reunirán en octubre para tartar temas 'sensibles,'" 26 agosto 2010, <http://elespectador.com/noticias/politica/articulo-221061-culmino-encuentro-entre-cancilleres-de-colombia-y-ecuador>

[174] Bill Van Auken, "Colombian high court rejects US bases agreement," *World Socialist Web Site*, 21 August 2010, <http://www.wsws.org/articles/2010/aug2010/colo-a21.shtml>

[175] *El Tiempo*, "Gobierno dice que 'no habrá verificación sobre presencia de FARC y Eln en Venezuela," 11 agosto 2010, <http://www.eltiempo.com/archivo/documento/CMS-7858074>

[176] *Semana*, "Santos establecerá una reacción común con México y Perú si EE.UU. legaliza marihuana," 25 agosto 2010, <http://www.semana.com/noticias-mundo/santos-establecera-reaccion-comun-mexico-peru-eeuu-legaliza-marihuana/143548.aspx>

[177] *RCN Radio*, "Estados Unidos busca frenar la corrupción en Colombia," 7 octubre 2010, <http://www.rcnradio.com/node/50564>

[178] Adriaan Alsema, "US drug czar to meet Uribe," *Colombia Reports*, 28 September 2009, <http://colombiareports.com/colombia-news/news/6132-us-drug-czar-to-meet-uribe.html>

[179] Niccolò Machiavelli, *The Discourses*, trans. Leslie J. Walker, S. J. (London: Penguin, 1998), 122-3.

[180] Niccolò Machiavelli, *The Prince* , trans. Luigi Ricci (New York: Signet, 1999), 35. Machiavelli, *The Discourses*, 276, 277, 400.

[181] Machiavelli, *The Prince*, 37. Machiavelli, *The Discourses*, 222.

[182] Machiavelli, *The Discourses*, 124-5, 126.

[183] Machiavelli, *The Prince*, 97.

[184] Machiavelli, *The Prince*, 94.

[185] Machiavelli, *The Prince*, 88, 95, 98.

[186] Machiavelli, *The Prince*, 36.

[187] Machiavelli, *The Prince*, 93.

[188] Machiavelli, *The Discourses*, 426, 428, 429.

[189] Machiavelli, *The Prince*, 32, 38, 83. Machiavelli, *The Discourses*, 466.

[190] Machiavelli, *The Prince*, 58. Machiavelli, *The Discourses*, 463.

[191] Machiavelli, *The Discourses*, 113, 116.

[192] Machiavelli, *The Discourses*, 116.

[193] Machiavelli, *The Discourses*, 116.

[194] Machiavelli, *The Discourses*, 114-5.

[195] Machiavelli, *The Discourses*, 107, 108.

[196] Machiavelli, *The Discourses*, 155.

[197] Machiavelli, *The Prince*, 53, 83.

[198] Machiavelli, *The Discourses*, 282-3.

[199] Machiavelli, *The Prince*, 34, 65. Machiavelli, *The Discourses*, 155.

[200] Machiavelli, , *The Prince*, 97.

[201] Machiavelli, *The Prince*, 62. Machiavelli, *The Discourses*, 114.

[202] Machiavelli, *The Discourses*, 494, 495.

[203] Machiavelli, *The Prince*, 65.

[204] Machiavelli, *The Prince*, 96.

[205] Machiavelli, *The Prince*, 96-7.

[206] Machiavelli, *The Prince*, 108.

[207] Machiavelli, *The Discourses*, 215.

[208] Machiavelli, *The Prince*, 108.

[209] Machiavelli, *The Prince*, 67, 53, 72. Machiavelli, *The Discourses*, 375, 495.

[210] Machiavelli, *The Prince*, 123.

[211] Machiavelli, *The Prince*, 302-3, 310.

[212] Machiavelli, *The Discourses*, 343, 442

[213] Antonio Gramsci, *Selections from the Prison Notebooks* (New York: International Publishers, 1971), 249.

[214] Gramsci, 169-170.

[215] Gramsci, 244.

[216] Gramsci, 171.

[217] Gramsci, 261.

[218] Gramsci, 263.

[219] Gramsci, 137.

[220] Gramsci, 177.

[221] Gill, 56.

[222] Gill, 61.

[223] Gramsci, 210.

[224] Quote found in Margerite Feitlowitz's book, *A Lexicon of Terror: Argentina and the Legacies of Torture*, 3. Laura Yusem, director, *Paso de dos;* Buenos Aires, 1990

[225] Herbert Braun, *Our Guerrillas, Our Sidewalks*, 177

[226] Pav Jordan, "Growing Pains in Colombia vex Canadian mining companies," *Business Without Borders*, 9 August 2012. < http://www.bwob.ca/industries/natural-resources/growing-pains-in-colombia-vex-canadian-mining-companies/ >

[227] Human rights activist and member of the Association of Indigenous Councils of Cauca in Colombia.

[228] Interview with Manuel Rozental, "Indigenous Community in Colombia Fears Start of 'Dirty War,'" *Democracy Now!* 20 May 2005. <http://www.democracynow.org/2005/5/20/indigenous_community_in _colombia_fears_start>

[229] Nazih Richani, "Caudillos and the Crisis of the Colombian State: fragmented sovereignty, the war system and the privatisation of counterinsurgency in Colombia," *Third World Quarterly*, Vol 28, No. 2, 2007, p. 405.

[230] Miguel Eduardo Cárdenas Rivera and Felipe Díaz Chavez, "Hegemonía en Colombia: caracterización y alternativas frente al poder global," *Utopía y Praxis Latinoamericana*, Año 16, No 53 (Abril-Junio, 2011), pp13 - 26.

[231] Marco Palacios. 2006. *Between Legitimacy and Violence: A History of Colombia, 1875-2002*, Durham and London: Duke University Press, p. 265.

[232] Mohammed Ayoob, "Subaltern Realism: International Relations Theory Meets the Third Word," *International Relations Theory and the Third Word*, Edited by Stephanie G. Neuman, (New York: St. Martin's Press, 1998) p. 46.

[233] Colombia is divided by three major mountain ranges, bordering two oceans, the Amazon jungle, among other physical impediments.

[234] Alex McDougall, "State Power and Its Implications for Civil War Colombia," *Studies in Conflict & Terrorism*, 32: 2009. Pp. 340-341.

[235] Robert W. Cox, *The Political Economy of a Plural World: Critical reflections on Power, Morals and Civilizations* (London: Routledge, 2002), p. 167.

[236] Cox, 174.

[237] Martin, Amanda; Nygard, Kath. "Faces of Colombia: Who are the Victims of Free Trade?" *Witness for Peace Colombia Team* <http://www.witnessforpeace.org/downloads/FacesofColombiaFTAfinal.pdf>

[238] Secretariado del Estado Mayor Dentral de las FARC-EP, "Manuel Vivo," Official *FARC-EP* blog, 26 March 2013, < http://farc-ep.co/?p=2220 >

[239] Milton Friedman, "Chap. 1: The Relation between Economic Freedom and Political Freedom," *Capitalism and Freedom*, 1962, page 4, <http://www.ditext.com/friedman/cf1.html> (10 January 2008), 1, 4.

[240] Friedman, 4.

[241] Friedman, 4.

[242] Friedman, 1-2.

[243] Friedman, 4.

[244] Friedman, 3.

[245] Francis Fukuyama, "The End of History?" in *The Geopolitics Reader, Second Edition*, ed. Gearoid O. Tuathail, Simon Dalby, Paul Routledge (London: Routledge, 2006), 107. Article originally published in *National Interest*, # 16, 1989.

[246] Fukuyama, 107.

[247] Fukuyama, 109.

[248] Fukuyama, 113.

[249] George W. Bush, "National Security Strategy of the United States of America," 2002, Introduction page 2. <http://www.whitehouse.gov/nsc/nss.pdf>

[250] Bush, 18.

[251] Bush, 17.

[252] Bush, 29.

[253] Karl Polany, *The Great Transformation: The Political and Economic Origins of Our Time* (Boston: Beacon Press, 2001), 35, 39, 42, 72, 74, 132, 145, 148, 155.

[254] David Harvey, *A Brief History of Neoliberalism* (Oxford: University Press, 2007), 38.

[255] Polanyi, 71-72, 75, 79.

[256] Amy Chua, *World on Fire: How Exporting Free Market Democracy Breeds Ethnic Hatred and Global Instability* (Doubleday, 2003).

[257] Polanyi, 151, 156, 169-171.

[258] Asad Ismi, *Profiting from Repression: Canadian Investment in and Trade with Colombia, 3rd Edition*, April 2012. Commissioned and Published by The Canadian Union of Postal Workers. P. 4.

[259] Territory is also valuable for strategic military purposes.

[260] John Otis, "If Colombia Is Winning Its War, Why the Fleeing?" *Time*, 1 September 2010, <http://www.time.com/time/world/article/0,8599,1919758,00.html?xid =rss-topstories>

[261] Colombian Ministry of Defence, "Virtuous Circle," Annual Report.

[262] MiningWatch Canada: Suppressed Report Confirms International Violations by Canadian Mining Companies (2010).

[263] Canada's Coalition to End Global Poverty. Americas Policy Group:"Briefing Note: Mining" (2012); Peace Brigades International Colombia: Mining in Colombia: At what Cost? (2011); The Walrus: The Only Risk is Wanting to Stay (2011).

[264] Canadian Network for Corporate Accountability: Comments on the Implications of the Guiding Principles for the Implementation of the United Nations Framework for CSR in the Canadian Extractive Sector (2011).

[265] FARC and ELN, "Comunicado," 31 March 2013. < http://farc-ep.co/?p=2228 > 1 April 2013

[266] Olle Ohlsen Pettersson, "FARC, ELN 'join forces' to fight foreign companies," *Colombia Reports*, 1 April 2013. < http://www.colombiareports.com/colombia-news/news/28761-farc-eln-join-forces-to-fight-foreign-companies.html >

[267] FARC and ELN, "Comunicado," 31 March 2013. < http://farc-ep.co/?p=2228 > 1 April 2013

[268] Michel Foucault, *Power*, 2.

[269] Foucault, *Power*, 3.

[270] Foucault, *Power*, 5, 7-8.

[271] Foucault, *Power*, 10.

[272] Foucault, *Power*, 12.

[273] Foucault, *Power*, 13, 14.

[274] Foucault, *Power*, 14, 32, 51, 52.

[275] Foucault, *Power*, 131-132.

[276] Foucault, *Power*, 132.

[277] James F. Rochlin, *Social Forces and the Revolution in Military Affairs: The Cases of Colombia and Mexico*, Manuscript before publication, 2007 copy, 3.

[278] Foucault, *Power*, 132-133.

[279] Foucault, *Power*, 133.

[280] Foucault, *Discipline and Punish*, 110, 113.

[281] Foucault, *Discipline and Punish*, 138, 142-143.

[282] Foucault, *Discipline and Punish*, 164, 182-184.

[283] Foucault, *Discipline and Punish*, 201, 206-208, 218.

[284] Foucault, *Discipline and Punish*, 25-26.

[285] Colonel Gabriel Pinilla (Colombian Army), "Are we approaching the read defeat of the FARC?" U.S. War College, International Fellow, Class of 2009, Master's of Strategic Studies Strategy Research Project, 26-28.

[286] Ann Mason, "Colombia's Democratic Security Agenda: Public Order in the Security Tripod," *Security Dialogue*, December 2003, Vol. 34, Issue 4, 407.

Made in the USA
Middletown, DE
17 September 2020

19844382R00124